First Published in 1979 by
Sampson Low, Berkshire House,
Queen Street, Maidenhead,
Berkshire SL6 1NF

SBN 562 00119 0

Designed by Peter Kenny Ltd., Ewell
Filmset by Tradespools Ltd., and Filmtype Services Ltd.
Printed by Waterlows (Dunstable) Ltd.

AUDREY ELLIS

Dinner

MENUS

MENU PLANNERS

Sampson Low

Dinner MENUS

Contents

8
Smoked mackerel with brown bread and butter
Tripe Italienne
Buttered noodles
Broad beans
Raspberry soufflé

thirty

9
Boiled dinner New England style
Oven-baked potatoes
Black cherry clafouti

thirty two

10
Salade Niçoise
Fillet of pork en croûte
Cauliflower with white sauce
Fruit salad with Cointreau

thirty four

11
Damascus golden chicken
Lemon saffron rice
Cucumber and yogurt raitha
Carrot and pepper sticks
Blintzes

thirty six

12
Smoked haddock pâté
Poulet à la moutarde
Savoury vegetable medley
Almond mousse

thirty eight

13
Summer lettuce soup
Crown roast of lamb
Roast potatoes
Apricot mallow

forty

14
Pâté of pork with walnuts
Melba toast
Chicken with sesame seeds
Chocolate and peppermint soufflé

forty two

15
Rhubarb soup
Royal marmalade-glazed duck
Sweet and sour baby turnips
Cream puffs with raspberry syrup

forty four

16
Whittington's whitebait
Roast beef with roast potatoes
Honeyed carrots
Peach and rice custard

forty six

17
Fresh green pea soup
Roast pork with sweetcorn medley
Creamed potatoes
Blackcurrant soufflé

forty eight

18
Southern fried chicken on saffron rice
Fried aubergines
Raspberry mousse
Apple and grape platter

fifty

19
Smoked fish cream
Strasbourg style goose
Parslied boiled potatoes
Exotic fruit salad

fifty two

20
Jerusalem soup
Turkey with claret sauce
Roast parsnips and Brussels sprouts
Toasted apple pudding with brandied cream

fifty four

21
Chilled grapefruit halves
Baked hare with cranberries and chestnuts
Oven-baked potatoes and braised celery
Raisin lattice pie

fifty six

22
Hot consommé
Colonial goose
Roast potatoes, onion rings and carrots
Apple and chestnut charlotte

fifty eight

23
Avocado starters
Gingered autumn chicken
Pasta shells
Plum fritters
Red wine sauce

sixty

24
Apple and avocado salad
Chicken curry Veronique
Fluffy boiled rice
Saucy lemon pudding and cream

sixty two

25
Cream of chestnut soup
Pigeon with orange sauce
Red cabbage and carrot layer
Chocolate cups with ginger cream

sixty four

26
Cauliflower and bacon ramekins
Game pie
Sovereign salad
Grapefruit Alaska

sixty six

27
Tomato juice cocktail
Roast pheasant
Frosted Brussels sprouts with croûtons
Fresh lime mousse
Devils on horseback

sixty eight

28
Golden pumpkin soup
Roast goose with apple and raisin stuffing
Floury boiled potatoes
Red cabbage
Damson cheesecake

seventy

29
Grilled grapefruit
Creamed turkey duchesse
Decorated ice cream dessert
Gaelic coffee

seventy two

Cook's guide

In this book, quantities are given in Metric, Imperial and American measures. Where ingredients are differently described in the U.S.A., the alternative name is given in brackets. All menus are to serve 4 unless otherwise indicated.

Spoon measures: In general, teaspoons and table-spoons make handy measures, although not always completely accurate. 3 teaspoons equal 1 tablespoon and 8 tablespoons equal about 150 ml/$\frac{1}{4}$ Imperial pint. (If you use a standard measuring spoon, it actually holds 17.7 ml) The American tablespoon is slightly smaller (holding 14.2 ml) therefore occasionally an extra tablespoon is indicated in the American column of measures. All spoon measures are taken as being level.

Liquid measures: Quantities are given in millilitres, pints and American cup measures. The American pint contains only 16 fl oz compared with the Imperial pint which contains 20 fl oz, and the American measuring cup contains 8 fl oz.

Can sizes: Since there is no absolute conformity among manufacturers in their can sizes, the exact quantity required is indicated. If, for example, a 396 g/14 oz can of tomatoes is required, the nearest equivalent you can find on the shelves may be up to 50g/2 oz larger or smaller. Generally speaking, this does not affect the success of the recipe.

Oven temperature chart: Few ovens are accurately adjusted. If you are not satisfied with the results given by your oven, test the temperature range with an oven thermometer and set your dial accordingly.

Oven temperature chart

	°F	°C	Gas Mark
Very cool	225	110	
	250	130	$\frac{1}{2}$
Cool	275	140	1
	300	150	2
Moderate	325	170	3
	350	180	4
Moderately hot	375	190	5
	400	200	6
Hot	425	220	7
	450	230	8
Very hot	475	240	9

Dinner MENUS

Introduction

Dinner is the really important meal of the day for most families. It is served at an hour when everyone gets together and is able to devote plenty of time to enjoying the food. It is also the meal at which hostesses can show off their cooking prowess and offer their guests something special.

As there are usually three courses, planning needs to be more careful than for simpler meals. No cook wants a last-minute panic in the kitchen over the impossible task of bringing three delicate dishes to completion at the same time. It is usually easier to make the first course a cold one, or some kind of soup that can be left to look after itself, or heated up at the last minute.

Items which you can reasonably purchase and would take some trouble to prepare are suggested to round out the menus, so that you can devote yourself to some really interesting dishes. For instance, smoked mackerel is given as a starter where the main dish and its accompaniment require a lot of attention. In other cases, a simple dish is suggested where no recipe is needed such as 'sliced strawberries in white wine'. The idea, however, may be new to you and that is just the sort of inspiration I hope this book will provide.

Always make the preparation of dinner for a party easy for yourself by doing as much as possible in advance. Get the coffee tray ready with coffee measured and ready to perk, lay the table, chill the wine or open it to come up to room temperature if necessary. Then you will be in the right relaxed mood to enjoy the company of your guests.

Audrey Ellis

Serving wine and other drinks

Any food is enhanced by the drinks served with it and this is particularly true when choosing the right wine to marry up with certain dishes. The mood for a successful dinner is often set by the choice of aperitifs beforehand and it is much better to know exactly what you have to offer rather than enquire from guests what they would like to drink. This causes an awkward hesitation and may start the occasion off badly because, as luck would have it, their choice is not available!

Your stock of aperitifs

Nowadays, your range can be limited to one dry and one sweet sherry, gin with its various accompaniments, and dry and sweet vermouths. A small bottle of Angostura bitters enables you to offer a Pink Gin and dry vermouth can be mixed with gin to make a Dry Martini, or combined with an equal quantity of sweet vermouth. If you have vodka in your cupboard, suggest a vodka cocktail; a Bloody Mary is made with vodka, tomato juice and ice, and a Vodkatini with equal quantities of vodka and dry Martini. Campari diluted with soda is another popular choice. Few people would be unable to pick an enjoyable aperitif from this selection. Make sure you have the right glasses for these drinks ready and polished up, ice turned out of the trays into an insulated tub and a few thin lemon slices on a plate. For those who do not take alcohol, tomato juice with Worcestershire sauce, or orange juice would be good alternatives.

Table wines

Wine need not be expensive to be enjoyable, even to those who have some expertise on the subject, if correctly chosen and served. Most of the branded blended wines are consistently good and as they are bottled in large sizes you are unlikely to run short. A standard single bottle will really not serve four throughout a dinner party. It holds only five generous glasses whereas the popular litre size (35 fl oz/4½ cups) holds seven. Also, the best alternative for those who do not keep aperitifs on hand is to offer guests a glass of the wine they will be drinking with the meal immediately on arrival.

White wines: These are perhaps the most versatile of all since they are light enough to accompany almost any food successfully. There is one category of very sweet heavy white wines, only suitable to serve with the pudding or dessert. These should be only lightly chilled, whereas drier white wines require to be served very cold. For this reason, the correct glasses are long-stemmed so that you are not obliged to hold them by the bowl and thus warm the contents. The bottle should only be opened when you are ready to pour as the bouquet and fruitiness of such wines is soon dissipated by contact with the air. If possible, chill white wine in the door of the refrigerator for about 2 hours before it is needed. There are many sparkling white wines other than Champagne which cost a great deal less. They all have the advantage of being suitable to serve throughout a meal for both savoury and sweet dishes. They are better kept on ice and served in tulip-shaped glasses to conserve the sparkle as long as possible. The really festive ones are all described as *mousseux* but there are semi-sparkling wines of great charm labelled *pétillant*.

Red wines: The robustness of most red wines makes them unsuitable to be served with delicate starters, fish or white meat dishes, and desserts. An inexpensive red wine is probably less satisfactory than the white equivalent; those of low quality tend to taste both vinegary and peppery. A good red may be very expensive indeed and the quality will only be fully appreciated by those with an educated palate. Again, the service is all important. The younger and less developed in flavour, the longer the wine can be allowed to 'breathe' before serving; that is opened, and allowed to come in contact with the air. Short-stemmed glasses are recommended so that the drinker cups the bowl with his warm hand and encourages the release of the bouquet of the wine. As red wines should come up fully to room temperature before drinking and they sometimes have considerable sediment, bottles should be placed upright in a warm place in good time to allow any sediment to sink to the bottom and the wine to warm as much as is necessary. Very fine old red wines need little time to

'breathe' and they can be transferred to a decanter with a stopper. Less noble wines are often left open for 24 hours or more these days and for this reason are decanted into a carafe without a stopper.

Rosé wines: Coming as they do between white and red, and having some of the qualities of both, rosé wines are also considered suitable to serve throughout a meal. A sparkling rosé strikes a particularly convivial note. They should be served in white wine glasses and lightly chilled although not too cold.

Generally speaking, white wines will be served before reds, with a return to a sweet white with dessert. Although sherry is sometimes served with clear soups, the first wine is usually a dry white to go with the starter and with fish. If the next course is a white meat or a made-up dish in a cream sauce, the wine should be a medium dry white. Red wine is appropriate with red meats, game and made-up dishes in a brown sauce. The French fashion of serving cheese before the dessert allows red wine to be finished up with cheese, its perfect partner. After the meal, it is pleasant to continue drinking a sweet white wine with coffee instead of brandy or a liqueur.

Coffee and after-dinner drinks
Good coffee is the perfect conclusion to a well-chosen and prepared meal. Sometimes in the rush of getting ready it is forgotten until the moment it is required. But it is much wiser to set the coffee tray at the same time as laying the table. A small jug of single cream (half and half) and prettily coloured coffee sugar should be provided. Thicker cream sometimes will not pour when it has been standing for a while and it can also form fatty globules on top of the coffee. For special coffee confections, lightly whipped cream is essential. However you make your coffee, it should be completely clear and free from sediment (as it will be if made in a percolator or special coffee machine). If you make coffee by the jug method, use a warm jug, add 1 tablespoon of cold water to the made coffee, stir well and allow to stand for several minutes. Pour very carefully through a fine strainer into a warm serving jug without disturbing the sediment which should have sunk to the bottom. Arrange the conclusion of the meal so that you can serve the coffee really freshly made and hot. If you grind the beans yourself, you will be rewarded for this extra trouble by strong flavour without any hint of bitterness. When ground coffee is stale, adding extra to the brew only intensifies the bitter flavour.

If the meal has been a comparatively light one, petits fours, glacé fruits or crystallised ginger can be offered with the coffee. After-dinner mints or wafer-thin chocolate mints are also acceptable.

Most men seem to prefer brandy rather than a sweet liqueur to finish up the meal. Brandy should also be served warm and it has even been the custom to warm the glasses so that the aroma of the spirit is released by the warmth. That is why brandy is served in balloon glasses which can be cupped in the hand, swirled round and sniffed appreciatively. Liqueur glasses are usually like tiny port glasses and only a small quantity is drunk. Fruit-flavoured liqueurs are prime favourites but those flavoured with coffee, chocolate, spices or herbs are also popular. Liqueurs can be served as long drinks over crushed ice.

Non-alcoholic drinks
Fruit juices including orange, grapefruit, peach and apricot nectars, and blackcurrant and lime cordials, are possibles for guests who do not drink wine. These drinks taste much better and more sophisticated served over ice. Apple juice can be drunk as an alternative to cider. Light ale can be diluted with ginger ale or lemonade to make a shandy and lager diluted with lime. These mixtures are handy to offer those who prefer to take only a little alcohol, and can be served in tumblers or large wine glasses.

Punches and cups
The amount of spirits used governs the cost and the potency of a cup. Usually two or three measures of gin or brandy are added to a litre of wine. Then it is further diluted by adding a few measures of fruit juice and the same amount of fizzy lemonade or ginger ale as wine.

Dinner
MENUS

A few of these meal plans are for the family but most are intended to grace more elegant occasions with guests. It is nice to be able to serve unusual starters and many are included. Where the recipes suggested are simple, such as 'chilled melon wedges', no recipe is considered necessary to be given. The same rule applies to some sweets and desserts.

Originality has been the first consideration in the choice of recipes because it is more important to offer an appetising dish that is original than an expensive one which might equally well be enjoyed in a restaurant. And of course, deference has been paid to the practical side of catering, ensuring that much of the preparation for the meals can be done in advance.

MENU 1

Jellied consommé
Fresh salmon puff
Asparagus with mimosa topping
Sliced strawberries in white wine

Fresh salmon puff

INGREDIENTS	METRIC	IMP.	U.S.
Puff pastry [paste]	450 g	1 lb	1 lb
Cooked fresh salmon	175 g	6 oz	6 oz
Cooked white fish	225 g	8 oz	½ lb
Savoury white sauce	300 ml	½ pint	1¼ cups
Cooked rice	100 g	4 oz	¾ cup
2 tbspn chopped parsley			
1 tspn anchovy essence [extract]			
Beaten egg to glaze			
Lemon wedges			
Sprigs of watercress			

Roll out the pastry to a rectangle 14 inches/35 cm by 8 inches/20 cm. Cut triangles with 4 inch/10 cm sides off each corner. Mix together all ingredients for the filling and place down the centre of the pastry. Fold up the sides and pointed ends of the pastry to make a neat rectangle. Brush with beaten egg and seal the edges well together. Roll out pastry trimmings and cut into strips. Plait these together and use to cover the joins in the pastry envelope. Brush all over with beaten egg and place on a dampened baking sheet. Bake in a hot oven (450°F, 230°C, Gas Mark 8) for 10 minutes, then lower heat to moderately hot (375°F, 190°C, Gas Mark 5) for a further 30 minutes. Garnish with lemon wedges and sprigs of watercress.

Asparagus with mimosa topping

INGREDIENTS	METRIC	IMP.	U.S.
Trimmed asparagus spears	450 g	1 lb	1 lb
1 hard-boiled egg yolk			
Butter	50 g	2 oz	¼ cup
Soft white breadcrumbs	100 g	4 oz	1¼ cups
Salt and pepper			
1 tbspn finely chopped parsley			

If the asparagus spears are thin, the heads may drop off in cooking. Either steam them in a glass preserving jar, or cook upright in a deep sauce-pan with the heads just above the water. If cooking them lying flat in a shallow pan, cut a strip of foil wide enough to support the whole length of the trimmed asparagus spears and long enough to line the base of the pan and come far enough up the sides to provide handles to lift the cooked vegetables out of the pan. Pierce the middle of the strip so that when you lift the bundle, surplus water will drain away easily. Cooking time averages about 25 minutes but will depend on the thickness of the spears and the method of cooking. Mash the egg yolk with a fork. Melt three quarters of the butter and use to toss the crumbs until just turning golden and all the butter is absorbed. Remove from the heat, season to taste and stir in the egg yolk and parsley. Melt the remaining butter and cook until golden brown. Place the well-drained asparagus on a warm serving dish, pour the browned butter over the tips only. Spoon the topping over the asparagus.

Jellied consommé comes in cans and should be chilled in the refrigerator before the can is opened. Spoon it out into small soup coupes and break up gently with a fork. Serve well chilled, or the consommé will tend to melt and lose its shape and sparkle. If liked, serve with cheese straws.

Sliced strawberries in white wine make a quick, refreshing dessert. Using approximately 750 g/1½ lb strawberries, divide among individual dishes. Sugar lightly and pour 1 tablespoon white wine over each. Refrigerate for about 1 hour.

MENU 2

Pears with Liptauer cheese
Sole in Chablis sauce with spinach
Carrots and French beans
Redcurrant sorbet

Pears with Liptauer cheese

INGREDIENTS	METRIC	IMP.	U.S.
Demi-sel cheese	75 g	3 oz	3 oz
1 tbspn single cream [half & half]			
1 tspn capers			
1 tspn paprika pepper			
Salt and pepper			
2 large eating pears			
2 tspn French [Italian] dressing			
Few lettuce leaves			
½ cucumber, sliced			
2 stuffed green olives, halved			

First make the filling. Mash the cheese and cream with a fork, beat in the finely chopped capers, paprika and seasoning to taste. Peel, halve and core the pears and brush with the salad dressing to prevent discoloration. Arrange the pear halves, cut side uppermost, on individual plates on a bed of lettuce leaves and cucumber slices. Pipe or spoon the cheese mixture into the hollows and garnish each one with half a stuffed green olive.

Liptauer cheese can be used as a filling for avocado pears instead of the more usual prawns with oil and vinegar dressing. In this case, substitute black olives for stuffed green olives.

Redcurrant sorbet

INGREDIENTS	METRIC	IMP.	U.S.
Redcurrant purée	450 ml	¾ pint	2 cups —
1 tspn unflavoured gelatine [gelatin]			
2 egg whites			

Heat a little of the fruit purée and add the gelatine. Allow it to dissolve then add the remaining purée and stir well. Turn into a bowl, cover the surface with freezer cling-film and place in the freezer until the mixture has thickened. Remove, fold in the stiffly beaten egg whites. Refreeze.

Sole in chablis sauce with spinach

INGREDIENTS	METRIC	IMP.	U.S.
Spinach	*750 g*	*1½ lb*	*1½ lb*
Salt and pepper			
½ tspn ground mace			
4 large sole fillets			
2 tbspn chopped parsley			
Grated Gruyère [Swiss] cheese	*50 g*	*2 oz*	*½ cup*
SAUCE			
Butter	*40 g*	*1½ oz*	*3 tbspn*
Flour	*40 g*	*1½ oz*	*6 tbspn*
Single cream [half & half]	*150 ml*	*¼ pint*	*⅔ cup*
Chablis [dry white wine]	*75 ml*	*3 fl oz*	*6 tbspn*

Wash the spinach well, remove any coarse stems and cook in the water clinging to the leaves until limp. Drain well and chop finely. Squeeze all excess moisture out through the holes of the colander. Season to taste with salt, pepper and mace and spoon into a large shallow ovenproof dish. Skin the sole fillets, sprinkle the skin side with salt and parsley and roll up with that side inwards. Arrange the rolls on top of the spinach. To make the sauce, melt the butter, stir in the flour and cook gently for 1 minute. Add the cream and cook, stirring, until the sauce begins to thicken. Add the wine and salt to taste and bring to the boil, stirring constantly. Pour the sauce over the fish, leaving a border of spinach uncovered. Sprinkle with the cheese and bake in a moderate oven (350°F, 180°C, Gas Mark 4) for about 25 minutes, or until the sole is cooked.

MENU 3

Globe artichokes with lemon sauce
Halibut steaks with turmeric cream
Golden rice
Cherry crêpes flambées

Globe artichokes with lemon sauce

INGREDIENTS	METRIC	IMP.	U.S.
4 globe artichokes			
½ lemon			
Thick mayonnaise	150 ml	¼ pint	½ cup +
1 tbspn chopped tarragon			

Trim off the artichoke stalks and slice off tips of top leaves and points of tough outer leaves. Simmer in plenty of salted water, covered, until tender; about 35 minutes. When cooked an outer leaf can easily be detached. Drain well and allow to get cold. Pull out the centre mauve leaves, loosen the feathery chokes and remove them. Grate the lemon rind and squeeze the juice. Stir into the mayonnaise with the tarragon. Spoon some of the sauce into the centres of the artichokes and hand the rest separately.
Note: To eat artichokes hot with melted butter or cold with French dressing, pour a little of the preferred sauce on to the plate. Strip off leaves beginning from the outside, dip the fleshy base into the sauce and eat the base end only, placing discarded leaves on a side plate. Eat the artichoke bottom ('fond' in French) – with a fork.

Halibut steaks with turmeric cream

INGREDIENTS	METRIC	IMP.	U.S.
Long grain rice	175 g	6 oz	¾ cup
1 tspn powdered turmeric			
2 drops yellow food colouring			
2 small lemons			
4 halibut steaks			
Salt and pepper			
Length of cucumber	10 cm	4 inch	4 inch
Butter	25 g	1 oz	2 tbspn
Double [whipping] cream	150 ml	¼ pint	⅔ cup
4 sprigs mint			

Cook the rice in boiling salted water, with half the turmeric and the food colouring if liked. Drain and keep warm. Meanwhile, grate the rind from one lemon and squeeze the juice. Reserve one teaspoon of lemon juice and use the remaining juice to poach the fish steaks, plus just sufficient water to cover and seasoning to taste, for about 10 minutes, until tender enough for the flesh to separate easily from the bone. Drain the fish and keep hot. Slice the cucumber thickly, cut each slice into four and toss in the melted butter until limp. Cut the second lemon into quarters. Whip the cream with the remaining turmeric, salt, pepper and a few drops of reserved lemon juice. Arrange the fish steaks on a warm serving dish and pipe rosettes of seasoned cream down the centres. Sprinkle with grated lemon rind and place the cooked cucumber in the centre. Use the lemon quarters as dividers. Divide the rice between 4 individual dishes, and garnish with the tops of the mint sprigs. Chop the leaves and sprinkle over the cucumber. Serve at once.

Cherry crêpes flambées

INGREDIENTS	METRIC	IMP.	U.S.
8 thin pancakes			
Canned black cherries	425 g	15 oz	2 cups
1 tbspn lemon juice			
2 tbspn red currant jelly			
1 tbspn cornflour [cornstarch]			
Cherry brandy	50 ml	2 fl oz	$\frac{1}{4}$ cup
Cognac	50 ml	2 fl oz	$\frac{1}{4}$ cup
Vanilla ice cream or whipped cream			

Pancake batter can be very simple, based on allowing 1 egg to each 100 g/4 oz/1 cup plain (all-purpose) flour, and sufficient milk and water combined to make a thin pouring consistency. It can be enriched by using 2 eggs and all milk without the addition of any water as the liquid, and made lighter by stirring in 1 tablespoon or more of oil to the batter before cooking. Keep beating the batter as you cook the pancakes, otherwise the flour will tend to sink to the bottom and make the last one or two pancakes stodgy.

Make 8 pancakes using the richer recipe and separate them from each other with greaseproof paper. Store in the refrigerator until required. Drain the cherries, reserving the juice. Remove the stones. Bring the juice to the boil with the lemon juice and redcurrant jelly. Moisten the cornflour with a little cold water and gradually stir into the boiling juice. Reduce the heat and cook, stirring constantly, until the sauce thickens. Stir in the cherries. Set aside until required. At serving time, spoon a small amount of the cherry sauce into the centre of each pancake, fold into quarters and place in a chafing dish. Spoon the remaining cherry sauce around the filled pancakes. Heat through gently. Warm the cherry brandy and cognac in a small saucepan. Pour over the pancakes and set alight. Serve with ice cream or lightly whipped double cream.

MENU 4

Chilled fresh crab cocktails
Sweetbreads in cream
Minted new potatoes
Apricot crunch

WORK PLAN

1. Prepare crab for cocktails. Dice cucumber and toss in dressing.
2. Cook sweetbreads in stock for about 1 hour, or until tender. Trim and slice. Carry on with recipe for main dish up to the point of placing in the ovenproof dish. Prepare buttered crumbs.
3. Prepare apricots for sweet and place in pie dish.
4. Finish cocktails and chill.
5. Sprinkle crumbs over sweetbread mixture and place in oven to bake.
6. Scrape and cook potatoes with sprigs of mint.
7. Prepare topping for sweet, sprinkle over fruit, top with butter. Raise oven temperature and place in warmest area to bake.
8. Drain potatoes and keep warm. Serve crab cocktails.
9. Serve sweetbreads in cream with potatoes. Reduce oven heat to low.

Chilled fresh crab cocktails

INGREDIENTS	METRIC	IMP.	U.S.
1 fresh crab			
1 shredded lettuce			
Length cucumber	10 cm	4 inch	4 inch
2 tbspn French [Italian] dressing			
Double [whipping] cream	4 tbspn	4 tbspn	¼ cup
Mayonnaise	4 tbspn	4 tbspn	¼ cup

Boil the crab for 20 minutes, and cool. Place crab on its back, remove large and small claws. Remove 'flaps' or 'aprons'. Hold shell firmly in left hand, use right hand to pull out body from the shell. Remove gills, intestines and stomach. Carefully scrape out brown meat from shell discarding 'fingers' which are inedible. Crack large claws, remove white flesh, and chop roughly.

Half-fill cocktail glasses with shredded lettuce. Mix brown and white crab meats together. Cut the cucumber into fine dice, toss in the dressing and arrange on the lettuce in the centre, with crab meat round the edge. Mix the cream and mayonnaise together, use to mask the crab meat and place one small claw curved over the centre of each glass. Serve chilled.

Sweetbreads in cream

INGREDIENTS	METRIC	IMP.	U.S.
Butter	40 g	1½ oz	3 tbspn
Sliced button mushrooms	100 g	4 oz	1 cup
Flour	25 g	1 oz	¼ cup
Milk	150 ml	¼ pint	½ cup +
Sweetbread stock	300 ml	½ pint	1¼ cups
2 tbspn brandy			
Sliced cooked sweetbreads	450 g	1 lb	1 lb
Blanched almonds	25 g	1 oz	¼ cup
1 tbspn chopped parsley			
Single cream [half & half]	150 ml	¼ pint	⅔ cup
Salt and pepper			
Toasted breadcrumbs	25 g	1 oz	¼ cup

Heat 1 oz/25 g of the butter and use to cook the mushrooms until tender. Stir in the flour. Gradually add the milk and the hot meat stock and bring to the boil, stirring constantly. Add the brandy and fold in the sweetbreads, almonds, parsley and then the cream. Immediately remove from the heat, taste and adjust seasoning. Transfer to a well-greased ovenproof dish. Melt the remaining butter and stir in the crumbs until all the butter is absorbed. Sprinkle the buttered crumbs over the sweetbread mixture and stand the dish in a bain marie, or a roasting tin, half-filled with hot water. Bake in a moderate oven (350°F, 180°C, Gas Mark 4) for 30 minutes.

Apricot crunch

INGREDIENTS	METRIC	IMP.	U.S.
Apricots	1 kg	2 lb	2 lb
Soft [light] brown sugar	50 g	2 oz	¼ cup
Plain [all-purpose] flour	75 g	3 oz	¾ cup
Sugar	100 g	4 oz	½ cup
¼ tspn salt			
½ tspn ground cinnamon			
1 egg			
Melted butter	50 g	2 oz	¼ cup

Stone and quarter the apricots. Mix with the brown sugar. Spoon into an 8 inch/20 cm pie dish. Sieve the flour with the sugar, salt and cinnamon. Beat the egg lightly and add to the dry ingredients. Toss until the mixture is crumbly. Sprinkle over the apricots, drizzle with the melted butter and bake in a moderately hot oven (375°F, 190°C, Gas Mark 5) for 30 minutes. Serve warm with cream or custard sauce.

MENU

5

Deep-fried almond prawns
Cherry glazed ham
Sweet potato purée
Mixed salad
Californian cream

Sweet potato purée has a lovely golden colour and smooth texture. Canned sweet potatoes are almost orange in colour. There are two varieties of sweet potato; one pale in colour and rather mealy in texture, the other moist, soft and sugary. The latter is sometimes described as a yam and it is often easier to get canned yams than sweet potatoes. If using fresh sweet potatoes, cook whole in their skins in boiling salted water until tender (about 30 minutes). Drain the cooked potatoes well, peel and press through a sieve or mash thoroughly until smooth. Beat in hot milk a little at a time and season to taste with salt and pepper. To make the mixture richer, beat in a little butter, or use orange juice instead of hot milk in which case also add a little grated orange rind.

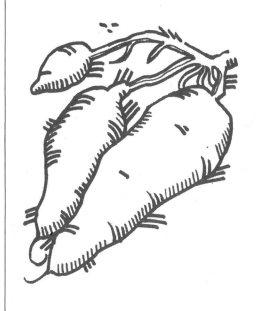

Deep-fried almond prawns

INGREDIENTS	METRIC	IMP.	U.S.
Fresh prawns [large shrimp]	450 g	1 lb	1 lb
Flour	50 g	2 oz	½ cup
¼ tspn white pepper			
¼ tspn ground coriander			
2 eggs			
1 tbspn cooking oil			
½ tspn soy sauce			
Ground almonds	75 g	3 oz	¾ cup
Fat for frying			

Shell the prawns, leaving the tail, and remove the back veins. Mix the flour, pepper and coriander. Dip each prawn into the flour mixture. Beat the eggs lightly and mix with the oil and soy sauce. Dip the flour-coated prawns into the egg mixture, and then into the ground almonds. Fry in hot deep fat for 3 minutes. Serve with lemon wedges or soy sauce.

Cherry glazed ham

INGREDIENTS	METRIC	IMP.	U.S.
Uncooked gammon joint [picnic shoulder]	2 kg	4 lb	4 lb
Beer	½ litre +	1 pint	2½ cups
Flour	1 kg	2 lb	8 cups
Water	750 ml	1¼ pints	3 cups
Canned cherry pie filling	275 g	10 oz	10 oz
4 tbspn rosé wine			
2 tbspn wine vinegar			
½ tspn dry mustard			
Pinch ground cloves			

Soak the joint in the beer overnight or for at least 12 hours. Remove and drain it. Mix together the flour and water to form a sticky dough and carefully mould this all round the joint, taking care to seal it completely. Place a wire rack over a baking tin half full of water and cover the rack with foil. Place the joint on top and bake in a hot oven (425°F, 220°C, Gas Mark 7) for 10 minutes. Reduce oven temperature to moderate (350°F, 180°C, Gas Mark 4) for 1½-2 hours. Meanwhile, mix together the pie filling, wine, wine vinegar, mustard and cloves and heat until well blended. Carefully remove the crust and discard it. Peel off the rind and fat from the joint. Pour the cherry sauce over the ham and return to the oven for a further 20 minutes.

Californian cream

INGREDIENTS	METRIC	IMP.	U.S.
Milk	300 ml	½ pint	1¼ cups
Unflavoured gelatine [gelatin]	15 g	½ oz	1 tbspn
2 eggs, separated			
Castor [granulated] sugar	75 g	3 oz	6 tbspn
¼ tspn salt			
4 tbspn sweet sherry			
1 tspn finely grated lemon rind			
Double [whipping] cream	150 ml	¼ pint	⅔ cup
Chopped candied fruits	75 g	3 oz	½ cup
Marzipan fruits to decorate			

Place the milk in a saucepan and sprinkle over the gelatine. Place over low heat and stir until the gelatine has dissolved. Remove from the heat. Whisk together the egg yolks, 1 oz/25 g of the sugar and the salt. Strain into the hot milk and cook over very low heat stirring constantly for 5 minutes, without allowing it to boil. Add the sherry and lemon rind and cool until the mixture begins to thicken. Beat the egg whites until stiff and gradually beat in the remaining sugar. Whip the cream, fold into the thickening mixture with the candied fruits. Finally fold in the egg whites gently to distribute fruits. Turn into a rinsed mould and allow to set. Turn out and decorate with marzipan fruits.

MENU
6

Chilled spinach soup
Cidered duckling with cherries
Fluffy boiled rice
Avocado fruit cocktails

Chilled spinach soup

INGREDIENTS	METRIC	IMP.	U.S.
Spinach	450 g	1 lb	1 lb
Butter	25 g	1 oz	2 tbspn
2 tbspn flour			
Milk	300 ml	$\frac{1}{2}$ pint	$1\frac{1}{4}$ cups
Salt and pepper			
Single cream [half & half]	150 ml	$\frac{1}{4}$ pint	$\frac{1}{2}$ cup

Cook the spinach in very little salted water. Drain well and chop finely. Melt the butter, stir in the flour, add the milk and bring to the boil, stirring constantly. Add the spinach, cook for 3 minutes and season to taste. Remove from the heat, stir in the cream, cool and serve chilled.

Cidered duckling with cherries

INGREDIENTS	METRIC	IMP.	U.S.
2 small ducklings			
Seasoned flour			
Butter	25 g	1 oz	2 tbspn
2 tbspn oil			
Dry cider	300 ml	$\frac{1}{2}$ pint	$1\frac{1}{4}$ cups
Stoned [pitted] cherries	225 g	8 oz	$\frac{1}{2}$ lb
Salt and pepper			
Double [whipping] cream	150 ml	$\frac{1}{4}$ pint	$\frac{1}{2}$ cup

Cut each duckling in half and coat with seasoned flour. Fry in the butter and oil until well browned on both sides. Transfer to a large baking dish. Pour the pan juices and the cider over the duckling halves. Cover with foil and bake in a moderately hot oven (400°F, 200°C, Gas Mark 6) for 35 minutes. Surround the duckling halves with the cherries, adding more cider if necessary. Cover and continue baking until the cherries are tender. Transfer the duckling halves and cherries to a warm serving platter. Strain the cooking liquid, bring to the boil and adjust the seasoning. Stir in the cream and reheat gently. Pour the sauce over the duckling halves.

Avocado fruit cocktails

INGREDIENTS	METRIC	IMP.	U.S.
Sugar	225 g	8 oz	1 cup
Water	300 ml	$\frac{1}{2}$ pint	$1\frac{1}{4}$ cups
2 large yellow-fleshed peaches			
2 medium avocados			
Grapes	100 g	4 oz	$\frac{1}{4}$ lb
Strawberries	100 g	4 oz	$\frac{1}{4}$ lb
2 tbspn lemon juice			
4 tbspn clear honey			

Dissolve the sugar in the water over gentle heat then boil for 2 minutes. Pour boiling water over the peaches to loosen the skins and remove them. Halve, remove the stones and slice the peaches into the hot sugar syrup. Chill. Peel the avocados, remove the stones and slice the flesh thinly. Halve and deseed the grapes. Place a few peach slices in the bases of 4 stemmed glasses. Mix together the remaining fruits, pile up decoratively in the glasses and spoon over a little syrup from the peaches. Mix together the lemon juice and honey and warm until well blended. Spoon over the cocktails and serve with small almond biscuits.

MENU 7

Chilled melon wedges
Mushroom and kidney sauté
Petits pois and sweetcorn
Strawberry almond flan

Mushroom and kidney sauté

INGREDIENTS	METRIC	IMP.	U.S.
8 button onions			
6 lambs' kidneys			
Butter	50 g	2 oz	$\frac{1}{4}$ cup
Chipolata sausages [small pork links]	225 g	8 oz	$\frac{1}{2}$ lb
Button mushrooms	225 g	8 oz	$\frac{1}{2}$ lb
1 tbspn flour			
1 chicken stock [bouillon] cube			
Boiling water	450 ml	$\frac{3}{4}$ pint	$1\frac{3}{4}$ cups
2 tspn tomato purée [paste]			
3 tbspn dry sherry			
1 bay leaf			
Fried bread croûtons			

Simmer the onions in a little boiling water for 5 minutes, then drain. Wash and skin the kidneys. Halve them and remove the cores. Melt the butter in a large pan and use to fry the kidneys, sausages and mushrooms until golden brown. Remove from the pan and keep hot. Stir the flour into the pan juices and cook gently for 2 minutes. Dissolve the stock cube in the boiling water and gradually add to the pan. Bring to the boil, stirring constantly, and cook until the sauce is smooth and slightly thickened. Stir in the tomato purée, sherry and bay leaf. Replace the kidneys, sausages and mushrooms in the pan and add the onions. Bring back to the boil, cover and simmer gently for about 20 minutes. Discard the bay leaf. Turn mixture into a heated serving dish and garnish with fried bread croûtons.

Strawberry almond flan

INGREDIENTS	METRIC	IMP.	U.S.
SWEET PASTRY			
Hard margarine	75 g	3 oz	⅓ cup
Plain [all-purpose] flour	175 g	6 oz	1½ cups
Castor [granulated] sugar	50 g	2 oz	¼ cup
1 egg yolk			
About 1 tbspn cold water to mix			
FILLING			
Margarine	50 g	2 oz	¼ cup
Castor [granulated] sugar	100 g	4 oz	½ cup
'Philly' soft cheese	75 g	3 oz	3 oz
2 eggs			
Few drops almond essence [extract]			
Ground almonds	50 g	2 oz	½ cup
Plain [all-purpose] flour	50 g	2 oz	½ cup
1 egg white			
Strawberries	100 g	4 oz	¼ lb
2–3 tbspn sieved strawberry jam			

To make the pastry, rub the margarine into the flour until the mixture resembles fine breadcrumbs. Add the sugar and egg yolk and enough water to make a pliable dough. Chill while you make the filling. Cream the margarine and sugar until light and fluffy and gradually beat in the 'Philly'. Add the whole eggs, one at a time, beating the mixture well after each addition. Beat in a few drops of almond flavouring. Fold in the almonds and flour. Whisk the egg white and fold into the mixture. Roll out the pastry on a well-floured board and use to line a 20 cm/8 inch flan tin or shallow cake tin. Pour in the filling mixture and use pastry trimmings to make a lattice design on the top. Bake in a moderately hot oven (400°F, 200°C, Gas Mark 6) for about 35 minutes, until golden brown. Cool, then decorate with strawberries. Heat the sieved jam and use to glaze the flan.

MENU 8

Smoked mackerel
with brown bread and butter
Tripe Italienne
Buttered noodles   Broad beans
Raspberry soufflé

Tripe Italienne

INGREDIENTS	METRIC	IMP.	U.S.
Tripe	450 g	1 lb	1 lb
Milk	150 ml	¼ pint	½ cup
Water	450 ml	¾ pint	1¾ cups
2 tspn salt			
1 large onion			
2 tbspn cooking oil			
2 tbspn tomato purée [paste]			
Dry white wine	150 ml	¼ pint	½ cup
Water	300 ml	½ pint	1¼ cups
1 bay leaf			
Pinch dried oregano			
Pinch grated nutmeg			
¼ tspn garlic salt			
¼ tspn freshly ground black pepper			
Few drops Worcestershire sauce			
Frozen green peas	100 g	4 oz	¼ lb

Simmer the tripe in the milk, water and salt for 1 hour. Drain and discard the cooking liquid. Cut the tripe into narrow strips. Slice the onion and fry in the oil until limp, but not browned. Add the cooked tripe, tomato purée, wine, water, bay leaf, oregano and seasonings. Simmer for 1 hour, adding more water during cooking if necessary. Stir in the green peas and simmer for a few minutes longer until the peas are cooked. Serve over steamed rice or noodles.

Raspberry soufflé

INGREDIENTS	METRIC	IMP.	U.S.
Raspberries	450 g	1 lb	1 lb
2 tspn gelatine [gelatin]			
4 tbspn water			
4 eggs			
Castor [granulated] sugar	100 g	4 oz	½ cup
Double [whipping] cream	300 ml	½ pint	1¼ cups
Chopped toasted nuts	50 g	2 oz	½ cup
5 walnut halves			

Reserve 4 of the best raspberries for decoration and sieve the remainder. Prepare a 15 cm/6 inch soufflé dish with a band of non-stick cooking parchment round the sides to come well above the top edge of the dish. Dissolve the gelatine in the water in a basin over a pan of hot water. Cool. Separate the eggs and whisk the yolks with the sugar and raspberry purée until the mixture forms a thick mousse. Whisk in the dissolved gelatine. When the mixture begins to thicken, whip half the cream until soft peaks form and fold in lightly. Whisk the egg whites until stiff, add to the raspberry mixture and fold in. Turn into the prepared dish and chill until set. Remove the paper and press chopped nuts around the exposed sides of the soufflé. Whip the remaining cream, pipe on top and decorate with walnuts and the reserved raspberries.

30

Boiled dinner New England style
Oven-baked potatoes
Black cherry clafouti

Boiled dinner New England style

INGREDIENTS	METRIC	IMP.	U.S.
Piece of brisket of beef	*450 g*	*1 lb*	*1 lb*
Roasting chicken	*1.75 kg*	*3½ lb*	*3½ lb*
1 chicken stock [bouillon] cube			
1 beef stock [bouillon] cube			
½ tspn dried mixed herbs			
¼ tspn ground mixed spices			
Carrots	*450 g*	*1 lb*	*1 lb*
1 small savoy cabbage			
1 small swede [rutabaga]			
Medium onions	*450 g*	*1 lb*	*1 lb*
Salt and pepper			

Put the trimmed beef with the chicken in a deep oval casserole with the stock cubes, herbs and spices. Cover with water to half the depth of the chicken, cover and simmer for 30 minutes. Quarter the carrots and cabbage and cut the swede into chunks. Add the carrots, onions and swede to the casserole, cover and cook for 40 minutes. Add the cabbage and cook for a further 20 minutes. Adjust seasoning. Serves 6.

Black cherry clafouti

INGREDIENTS	METRIC	IMP.	U.S.
Black [bing] cherries	1 kg	2 lb	2 lb
4 eggs			
Castor [granulated] sugar	150 g	5 oz	$\frac{2}{3}$ cup
2 tbspn flour			
1 tspn vanilla essence [extract]			
2 tbspn rum			
Milk	100 ml	3 fl oz	$\frac{1}{2}$ cup −
2 tbspn double [whipping] cream			

Stone the cherries and place in a buttered shallow ovenproof flan dish. Beat the eggs, sugar and flour together until foamy, then gradually beat in the vanilla essence, rum, milk and cream until the mixture is like a thin pancake batter. Pour over the cherries and bake in a moderately hot oven (375°F, 190°C, Gas (Mark 5) for 40 minutes. Serve warm. Serves 6.

Salade Niçoise
Fillet of pork en croûte
Cauliflower with white sauce
Fruit salad with Cointreau

Fillet of pork en croûte

INGREDIENTS	METRIC	IMP.	U.S.
2 pork fillets [tenderloins]			
2 tbspn oil			
Beaten egg to glaze			
PASTRY			
Plain [all-purpose] flour	*225 g*	*8 oz*	*2 cups*
Pinch salt			
Firm butter	*175 g*	*6 oz*	*¾ cup*
Cold water	*150 ml*	*¼ pint*	*½ cup+*
Few drops lemon juice			
STUFFING			
Fresh white breadcrumbs	*100 g*	*4 oz*	*1 cup*
2 tbspn chopped mixed herbs			
Grated rind and juice of 1 orange			
1 egg			
Salt and pepper			

Salade Niçoise Tear up the leaves of a large lettuce. Wash and drain well. Shake dry. Drain the oil from a small can of anchovies. Use the oil to make a vinaigrette dressing. Chop the anchovies. Chop a hardboiled egg. Combine the anchovies, egg, and dressing with 12 black olives. Divide the torn lettuce between four small glass dishes and spoon in the anchovy mixture.

Fruit salad with Cointreau Prepare fresh or canned pineapple cubes, peach slices, fresh orange segments and black grapes. Skin the peaches. Peel the grapes and remove the pips. Combine the fruits in a serving dish with juice and 1 tablespoon Cointreau (or more according to taste). Refrigerate for at least 1 hour before serving.

First make the pastry. Sift the flour and salt into a bowl. Cut the fat into pieces the size of a walnut and add to the flour mixture. Mix to a paste with the water and lemon juice. Using floured hands, shape pastry into an oblong and roll out thinly on a floured surface. Fold up the lower third of the pastry, bring the top third down on it and seal the edges. Turn with the fold on the left-hand side. Press lightly to flatten. Roll out again into a thin oblong and repeat this folding and flattening process. Chill for 20 minutes. Repeat the rolling, folding and resting processes as above three more times. Wrap in foil and chill for 1 hour. Meanwhile, combine all the ingredients for the stuffing, spread on the larger fillet, top with the smaller fillet and tie together firmly with string. Brush with oil and cook in a moderately hot oven (400°F, 200°C, Gas Mark 6) for 30 minutes. Cool and remove the string. Roll out the pastry to a thin square large enough to enclose the stuffed fillets. Trim neatly and reserve the trimmings. Roll these out again and cut pastry leaves to decorate. Enclose the stuffed fillets in a pastry parcel and seal the edges. Place on a damped baking sheet with the seal underneath, brush with beaten egg, arrange pastry leaves on top and brush again. Chill for 20 minutes. Cook in a hot oven (450°F, 230°C, Gas Mark 8) for 15 minutes, or until the pastry is golden brown, then reduce heat to moderately hot and cook for a further 15 minutes.

MENU 11

Damascus golden chicken
Lemon saffron rice
Cucumber and yogurt raitha
Carrot and pepper sticks
Blintzes

Damascus golden chicken

INGREDIENTS	METRIC	IMP.	U.S.
2 tbspn oil			
½ tspn ground cardamom			
½ tspn ground turmeric			
2 tbspn lemon juice			
1 tspn salt			
¼ tspn pepper			
Water	125 ml	4 fl oz	½ cup
Roasting chicken	1.5 kg	3½ lb	3½ lb
Shredded lettuce			
Orange wedges			
Sprigs of watercress			

Place the oil in a flameproof casserole or large saucepan and gradually blend in the cardamom, turmeric, lemon juice, salt, pepper and water. Heat gently, stirring all the time, until the mixture is smooth. Remove the skin from the chicken, place the bird in the pan and baste with the sauce. Cover tightly and simmer for 15 minutes. Repeat the basting and cooking process three times more, to give a total cooking time of 1 hour. It may be necessary to add a little more water during cooking. Place the chicken on a dish and spoon over the sauce remaining in the pan. Cool and chill. Serve on a bed of shredded lettuce, garnish with orange wedges and sprigs of watercress.

Blintzes

INGREDIENTS	METRIC	IMP.	U.S.
Plain [all-purpose] flour	100 g	4 oz	1 cup
1 tspn salt			
3 eggs			
Milk or water	225 ml	8 fl oz	1 cup
1 tbspn melted butter			
FILLING			
Cottage cheese	100 g	4 oz	¼ lb
Sultanas [golden raisins]	50 g	2 oz	⅓ cup

Sieve the flour and salt into a bowl. Beat in the eggs. Add the milk and beat until well blended. Spread a thin layer of the batter over the base of a lightly greased frying pan. Cook over low heat on one side only, until the top is dry. Turn out, cooked side up, on a clean tea towel. Continue until all the batter is made into thin pancakes. Fill each pancake with cottage cheese filling and fold as an envelope. Heat the pancakes in the melted butter. Serve with soured cream, cinnamon and sugar. Makes 10 blintzes.

Lemon saffron rice Cook 6 tablespoons long grain rice in boiling salted water until just tender. Drain well. Meanwhile steep a few saffron strands in 150 ml/¼ pint/½ cup boiling water. Strain, and use water to dissolve 1 chicken stock cube. Stir in 2 tablespoons lemon juice and 2 teaspoons grated lemon rind. Fold into the rice, turning gently to colour evenly. Leave to stand 15 minutes. Put 1 tablespoon oil in a clean pan, turn in the coloured rice. Place pan over a low heat, stirring until rice is heated through.

Cucumber and yogurt raitha Shred a 10 cm/4 inch length of cucumber finely. Place in a sieve to drain. Season 150 ml/¼ pint/½ cup natural (plain) yogurt with garlic salt and pepper. Stir in the drained cucumber. Turn into a small bowl. Sprinkle with chopped mint.

Smoked haddock pâté
Poulet à la moutarde
Savoury vegetable medley
Almond mousse

Smoked haddock pâté

INGREDIENTS	METRIC	IMP.	U.S.
Cooked smoked haddock [finnan haddie]	225 g	8 oz	½ lb
Juice of ½ lemon			
Cream cheese	75 g	3 oz	3 oz
Ground black pepper			
2 tbspn single cream [half & half]			
4 lemon slices			
4 parsley sprigs			
2 stalks celery			
2 medium carrots			

Flake the haddock and pound with the lemon juice. Beat in the cream cheese until smooth. Season to taste with black pepper and beat in the cream. Divide the mixture between 4 stemmed glass dishes, each placed on a saucer. Garnish the top with lemon twists and parsley. Cut the celery stalks into 1 inch/2 cm lengths and cut the carrots into very thin sticks. Arrange a ring of the vegetables decoratively around the base of each dish.

Poulet à la moutarde

INGREDIENTS	METRIC	IMP.	U.S.
Butter	50 g	2 oz	$\frac{1}{4}$ cup
4 chicken portions			
Dry white wine	7 tbspn	7 tbspn	$\frac{1}{2}$ cup
Bouquet garni			
Salt and freshly ground white pepper			
2 egg yolks			
2 tbspn soured cream			
2 tbspn Dijon mustard			
Pinch of cayenne pepper			
Watercress to garnish			

Melt the butter and use to fry the chicken portions until browned on all sides. Add the wine, bouquet garni and seasoning and bring to the boil. Cover and simmer gently for 25 minutes. Remove the chicken portions to a heated serving dish. Discard the bouquet garni. Mix together the egg yolks, cream, mustard and cayenne. Stir this into the gravy and reheat, stirring constantly, until the sauce thickens, but do not allow to boil. Pour the sauce over the chicken and garnish with watercress.

Savoury vegetable medley

INGREDIENTS	METRIC	IMP.	U.S.
Carrots	100 g	4 oz	$\frac{1}{4}$ lb
Turnip	100 g	4 oz	$\frac{1}{4}$ lb
Celeriac	100 g	4 oz	$\frac{1}{4}$ lb
White cabbage	225 g	8 oz	$\frac{1}{2}$ lb
1 leek			
Butter or margarine	50 g	2 oz	$\frac{1}{4}$ cup
Lean bacon	100 g	4 oz	$\frac{1}{4}$ lb
1 chicken stock [bouillon] cube			
Boiling water	300 ml	$\frac{1}{2}$ pint	$1\frac{1}{4}$ cups
Salt and pepper			
1 bay leaf			
Frozen green peas	50 g	2 oz	$\frac{1}{2}$ cup
Grated cheese	25 g	1 oz	$\frac{1}{4}$ cup

Peel and dice the carrots, turnip and celeriac. Roughly chop the cabbage. Wash and slice the leek. Melt the butter in a saucepan. Dice the bacon and fry the leek and bacon in the melted butter until the bacon is partially cooked. Add the prepared vegetables. Dissolve the stock cube in the boiling water. Add to the vegetables and bacon. Season with salt and pepper. Add the bay leaf; cover and simmer for 30 minutes. Add the peas and simmer, uncovered, for a further 5 minutes. Remove the bay leaf. Taste and adjust seasoning. Pile into a hot serving dish. Sprinkle with the grated cheese and place under a hot grill until the cheese begins to melt.

Almond mousse

INGREDIENTS	METRIC	IMP.	U.S.
Unflavoured gelatine [gelatin]	15 g	$\frac{1}{2}$ oz	1 tbspn
3 eggs			
Castor [granulated] sugar	100 g	4 oz	$\frac{1}{2}$ cup
Ground almonds	50 g	2 oz	$\frac{1}{2}$ cup
Few drops almond essence [extract]			
Double [whipping] cream	150 ml	$\frac{1}{4}$ pint	$\frac{2}{3}$ cup
Fruit pieces to decorate			

Dissolve the gelatine in 2 tablespoons water in a basin over a pan of hot water. Separate the eggs and whisk the yolks and sugar together until pale and thick. Fold in the almonds, a few drops of almond essence and the dissolved gelatine. Half whip the cream and fold into the almond mixture. Stiffly beat the egg whites and fold them in lightly. Spoon into sundae dishes and decorate with small pieces of fresh fruit.

Summer lettuce soup
Crown roast of lamb
Roast potatoes
Apricot mallow

Summer lettuce soup

INGREDIENTS	METRIC	IMP.	U.S.
1 large lettuce			
4 spring [green] onions			
Butter	25 g	1 oz	2 tbspn
2 tbspn flour			
Milk	600 ml	1 pint	2½ cups
1 tspn salt			
¼ tspn pepper			
¼ tspn dried tarragon			
1 egg yolk			
1 tbspn chopped mint			

Wash the lettuce and shred it. Chop the spring onions. Melt the butter in a saucepan. Add the lettuce and onion and cook gently for 5 minutes. Stir in the flour. Cook for 2-3 minutes. Remove from the heat and gradually add the milk and seasonings. Return to the heat and simmer covered, for 30 minutes. Liquidise in a blender, or sieve. Pour into a clean saucepan. Whisk in the egg yolk. Reheat gently but do not allow to boil. Pour into hot soup bowls and garnish with chopped mint.

To make a crown roast of lamb Cut the fat away 7.5 cm/ 3 inches in towards the eye of the meat across the whole best end of neck. Then trim down between the cutlet bones with a small knife, removing all meat and fat, so that the ends of the bones are left bare. Strip off the skin. Treat the other best end in the same way. With the point of the knife, make a slit between each cutlet and the next at the base, so that you can bring the two pieces of meat round, skin side inwards, each in a semi-circle, to meet and form a full circle. You must have pieces with at least 6 bones each to enable you to make the circle. Sew the ends together at one side, using a poultry needle (or a carpet needle) and fine string in two places – one near the base, the other just below the point to which the bones have been cleaned. Sew the other open ends together or secure with wooden skewers.

Crown roast of lamb

INGREDIENTS	METRIC	IMP.	U.S.
2 best ends of neck [racks] of lamb (6 bones each)			
1 packet parsley and thyme stuffing mix			
2 new carrots, grated			
Few cutlet frills			
Few glacé [candied] cherries			

Place the crown in a roasting tin, greased to prevent the joint from sticking. Make up the stuffing according to the directions, stir in the grated carrot, and spoon into the centre of the meat when it is in place in the roasting tin. Cover the tips of the bones with foil or greaseproof paper to prevent them from burning, and place in a moderately hot oven (375°F, 190°C, Gas Mark 5) for 1 hour and 10 minutes. Brush the top of the stuffing with juices from the pan halfway through cooking. If cooked empty, allow 10 minutes less cooking time. The centre can be filled with a small whole cooked cauliflower, or with mixed cooked diced vegetables. Top the bones with alternate cutlet frills and glacé cherries and serve with roast potatoes. Use the pan juices to make a thick gravy.

Apricot mallow

INGREDIENTS	METRIC	IMP.	U.S.
Apricots	450 g	1 lb	1 lb
Sugar to taste			
1 packet [package] orange jelly [jello]			
Evaporated milk	215 ml	7½ fl oz	1 cup
10 white marshmallows quartered			
Chopped angelica	50 g	2 oz	¼ cup

Halve the apricots and remove the stones. Poach the fruit in a little water with sugar to taste until just tender. Drain and reserve the syrup. Dissolve the jelly in a little boiling water and make up to ½ pint/300 ml/1¼ cups with apricot syrup. Allow to cool. Whisk the evaporated milk until thick and gradually whisk in the jelly. Chop the apricots, reserving a few for decoration, and fold into the jelly with the marshmallows and angelica. Turn into a 1 pint/ generous ½ litre/2½ cups mould and allow to set. Turn out on to a serving dish and decorate with the reserved apricot halves.

MENU 14

Pâté of pork with walnuts
Melba toast
Chicken with sesame seeds
Chocolate and peppermint soufflé

Pâté of pork with walnuts

INGREDIENTS	METRIC	IMP.	U.S.
Streaky [side] bacon slices	*175 g*	*6 oz*	*6 oz*
Lean pork	*675 g*	*1½ lb*	*1½ lb*
Belly of pork [fresh picnic shoulder]	*225 g*	*8 oz*	*½ lb*
Walnuts	*225 g*	*8 oz*	*2 cups*
1 small onion			
2 eggs			
Fresh brown breadcrumbs	*50 g*	*2 oz*	*1 cup*
¼ tspn ground mace			
½ tspn black pepper			
1 tspn salt			
2 tbspn brandy			
8 walnut halves			
Melted butter	*75 g*	*3 oz*	*⅓ cup*

Oil an earthenware dish or a 2 pint/1 litre/ 5 cup casserole. Line with the bacon rashers with the rinds removed. Mince the meat with the walnuts and onion until very fine. Beat the eggs lightly and add to the meat mixture along with the breadcrumbs, seasonings and brandy. Press into the prepared dish, cover with greaseproof paper or foil: put on the lid and stand the dish in a bain marie, or a roasting tin half filled with hot water. Bake in a moderate oven (350°F, 180°C, Gas Mark 4) for 3 hours. Remove the lid and place a light weight on top. Leave until cold. Remove paper and arrange the walnut halves on top. Pour over the melted butter. Store in the refrigerator.

Chicken with sesame seeds

INGREDIENTS	METRIC	IMP.	U.S.
Flour	75 g	3 oz	$\frac{3}{4}$ cup
Salt and pepper			
1 tbspn sesame seeds			
$\frac{1}{2}$ tspn ground coriander			
$\frac{1}{4}$ tspn ground ginger			
Pinch chilli powder			
4 chicken breasts			
Butter	75 g	3 oz	$\frac{1}{3}$ cup
1 tbspn olive oil			
Chicken stock [broth]	$\frac{1}{2}$ pint	300 ml	$1\frac{1}{4}$ cups
2 sprigs fresh rosemary, stripped			
3 tbspn dry white wine			
1 tbspn chopped parsley			
1 tbspn chopped watercress			
Double [whipping] cream	150 ml	$\frac{1}{4}$ pint	$\frac{1}{2}$ cup
Long grain rice	175 g	6 oz	1 cup
1 tbspn melted butter			

Season the flour with the salt, pepper, sesame seeds, coriander, ginger and chilli powder. Coat the chicken portions evenly. Fry the chicken portions in the butter and olive oil for 10 minutes on each side. Transfer the chicken to a warm dish and keep hot. Stir the remaining seasoned flour into the frying pan; add the chicken stock, rosemary and wine. Bring to the boil, simmer gently for 20 minutes, or until reduced by half. Add remaining chopped herbs to sauce. Stir in the cream and reheat gently. Cook the rice in boiling salted water for 12 minutes. Drain and rinse with hot water. Stir in the melted butter. Pile the rice into a serving dish and arrange the chicken portions on top. Hand the sauce in a sauceboat.

Chocolate and peppermint soufflé

INGREDIENTS	METRIC	IMP.	U.S.
Unflavoured gelatine [gelatin]	15 g	$\frac{1}{2}$ oz	1 tbspn
3 tbspn boiling water			
Plain [unsweetened] chocolate	100 g	4 oz	4 squares
2 tbspn milk			
Peppermint essence [extract]			
4 eggs, separated			
Castor [granulated] sugar	100 g	4 oz	$\frac{1}{2}$ cup
Double [whipping] cream	300 ml	$\frac{1}{2}$ pint	$1\frac{1}{4}$ cups
Chopped walnuts	40 g	$1\frac{1}{2}$ oz	$\frac{1}{4}$ cup
Few drops green food colouring			
4 chocolate peppermint creams			

Prepare the soufflé dish by tying a 4 inch/10 cm strip of siliconised parchment or foil around it. Ensure the paper stands 2 inches/5 cm above the edge of the dish. Dissolve the gelatine in the boiling water. Break up the chocolate and place in a basin over a pan of hot water. When melted blend in the milk and a few drops of peppermint essence. Whisk the egg yolks and sugar together until pale and very thick. Whisk in the dissolved gelatine and chocolate mixture. Allow to cool until just beginning to set. Whip the cream to the same consistency, retain a quarter for decoration and fold in the remainder. Whisk the egg whites until stiff and fold into the mixture. Pour into the prepared dish and chill until set. To serve, carefully remove the paper and gently press chopped nuts around the sides of the soufflé above the dish. Add one or two drops of peppermint essence and green food colouring to half the reserved whipped cream. Place the coloured cream in one side of a piping bag, and the plain cream in the other side so that two-coloured rosettes can be piped. Decorate the top edge of the soufflé with cream rosettes and arrange the halved peppermint creams in the centre.

MENU 15

Rhubarb soup
Royal marmalade-glazed duck
Sweet and sour baby turnips
Cream puffs with raspberry syrup

Rhubarb soup

INGREDIENTS	METRIC	IMP.	U.S.
Rhubarb	450 g	1 lb	1 lb
Water	900 ml	1½ pints	3¾ cups
1 cinnamon stick			
2 thin slices lemon			
Sugar	175 g	6 oz	¾ cup
2 tbspn cornflour [cornstarch]			
1 egg yolk			
Double [whipping] cream	150 ml	¼ pint	½ cup

Cut the rhubarb into 1 inch/2 cm pieces. Simmer in the water until tender. Drain through a sieve and discard the pulp. Simmer the rhubarb juice with the cinnamon stick, lemon slices and sugar until the sugar dissolves. Mix the cornflour with a little cold water and stir into the soup. Bring to the boil and simmer for 5 minutes, stirring continuously. Remove the cinnamon stick and lemon slices. Combine the egg yolk and double cream; stir into the hot soup. Heat through, but do not allow to boil. Serve hot with Melba toast.

Royal marmalade-glazed duck

INGREDIENTS	METRIC	IMP.	U.S.
Roasting duck	2.25 kg	5 lb	5 lb
1 tspn salt			
Marmalade	225 g	8 oz	1 cup
Dry sherry	150 ml	¼ pint	½ cup
Chicken stock [broth]	300 ml	½ pint	1¼ cups
1 tspn cornflour [cornstarch]			
Salt and pepper			
Parsley or watercress			

Prick the skin of the duck and sprinkle with the salt. Place the duck on a wire rack in a roasting pan and roast in a hot oven (425°F, 220°C, Gas Mark 7) for 30 minutes. Heat the marmalade and sherry until blended and brush one half of this mixture over the duck. Return the duck to a moderate oven (350°F, 180°C, Gas Mark 4) for 1½ hours. Mix a little of the stock with the cornflour and bring the remaining stock to the boil. Stir the cornflour paste into the stock and cook until thickened, stirring constantly. Stir the remaining marmalade and sherry mixture into the sauce. Season to taste with salt and pepper. Garnish the duck with parsley or watercress and hand the sauce in a sauceboat.

Sweet and sour baby turnips

INGREDIENTS	METRIC	IMP.	U.S.
Baby turnips	450 g	1 lb	1 lb
2 tbspn oil			
4 tbspn wine vinegar			
1 tbspn castor [granulated] sugar			
Salt and pepper			

Peel and dice the turnips. Heat the oil and use to sauté the turnip dice until golden. Stir in the vinegar, sugar, salt and pepper. Cover and cook over low heat until tender, shaking the pan occasionally to prevent them from sticking.

Cream puffs with raspberry syrup

INGREDIENTS	METRIC	IMP.	U.S.
Plain [all-purpose] flour	65 g	2½ oz	⅔ cup
Pinch salt			
Water	150 ml	¼ pint	½ cup +
Butter	50 g	2 oz	¼ cup
2 eggs			
Double [whipping] cream	150 ml	¼ pint	⅔ cup
Sugar to taste			
1 tbspn sherry			
SAUCE			
Sieved raspberries	225 g	8 oz	½ lb
Castor [granulated] sugar	100 g	4 oz	½ cup

First make the puffs. Sieve the flour and salt together. Put the water and butter into a saucepan and bring slowly to the boil. Remove from the heat and beat in the flour to form a ball which leaves the sides of the pan clean. Cool mixture to blood heat, then beat in the eggs, one at a time. Using a ½ inch/1 cm tube and large piping bag, force about 30 balls of paste, about the size of a walnut, on to wetted baking sheets. Bake in a moderately hot oven (375°F, 190°C, Gas Mark 5) for about 20 minutes, until crisp and pale golden brown. Cool on a wire rack. Whip the cream and sweeten to taste. Stir in the sherry and place in a piping bag with a small nozzle. Make a hole in the base of each puff and pipe in the flavoured cream. Meanwhile, mix together the raspberry purée and castor sugar. Heat slightly to dissolve the sugar. Pile the cream puffs in a glass serving dish and pour over the raspberry sauce.

MENU 16

Whittington's whitebait
Roast beef with roast potatoes
Honeyed carrots
Peach and rice custard

Whittington's whitebait

INGREDIENTS	METRIC	IMP.	U.S.
Flour	25 g	1 oz	$\frac{1}{4}$ cup
$\frac{1}{2}$ tspn paprika pepper			
Pinch cayenne pepper			
1 tspn salt			
Whitebait	450 g	1 lb	1 lb
Oil for frying			

Season the flour with the paprika, cayenne and salt and use to coat the whitebait twice. Cook the whitebait in a frying basket in deep hot oil for about 2 minutes until almost cooked, drain and reheat the oil until really hot. Plunge the fish in the oil again until golden brown. Drain well, serve with lemon wedges and brown bread and butter.

Honeyed carrots

INGREDIENTS	METRIC	IMP.	U.S.
4 large carrots			
Butter or margarine	50 g	2 oz	$\frac{1}{4}$ cup
1 tbspn made mustard			
Honey	50 ml	2 oz	$\frac{1}{4}$ cup
1 tbspn chopped almonds			

Peel and cut the carrots diagonally into 1 inch/ 25 mm slices. Cook in boiling salted water for 15 minutes. While the carrots are cooking, combine the butter, mustard and honey. Cook over low heat for 3 minutes until thoroughly blended. Drain the carrots. Pour the sauce over and sprinkle with the chopped almonds.

Peach and rice custard

INGREDIENTS	METRIC	IMP.	U.S.
Long grain rice	100 g	4 oz	$\frac{1}{2}$ cup
Milk	900 ml	$1\frac{1}{2}$ pints	4 cups
Pinch salt			
Castor [granulated] sugar	65 g	$2\frac{1}{2}$ oz	$\frac{1}{3}$ cup
2 eggs			
Few drops vanilla essence [extract]			
5 canned peach halves			
2 tbspns brown sugar			
Double [whipping] cream	150 ml	$\frac{1}{4}$ pint	$\frac{1}{2}$ cup+
Pinch ground cinnamon			

Place the rice, milk and salt in a pan. Bring to the boil, stirring constantly. As soon as the mixture is boiling, cover the pan and simmer for 45 minutes. Remove from the heat and stir in the sugar until dissolved. Beat the eggs with the vanilla essence, add a little of the hot rice mixture then pour into the pan and mix well. Cook for 1 minute, stirring all the time. Turn into a buttered ovenproof dish. Arrange the peach halves on top and sprinkle with almost all the brown sugar. Place under a hot grill until the sugar melts but watch carefully to prevent burning. Cool. When cold, whip the cream and use to decorate the custard. Sprinkle with the remaining sugar and the cinnamon.

MENU 17

Fresh green pea soup
Roast pork with sweetcorn medley
Creamed potatoes
Blackcurrant soufflé

Fresh green pea soup

INGREDIENTS	METRIC	IMP.	U.S.
2 chicken stock [bouillon] cubes			
1 tspn sugar			
Juice of ½ lemon			
1 large potato, sliced			
1 large onion, sliced			
1 large lettuce, shredded			
Green peas	700 g	1½ lb	1½ lb
Salt and pepper			
Double [whipping] cream	300 ml	½ pint	1¼ cups

Dissolve the stock cubes in 1 pint/generous ½ litre/2½ cups water, add the sugar, lemon juice, potato, onion, lettuce and peas. Bring to the boil, cover and simmer for 20 minutes. Sieve or liquidise the mixture and add a further 1 pint/generous ½ litre/2½ cups boiling water. Reheat and adjust seasoning. Stir in the cream and serve hot or cold. Serves 6.

Roast pork with sweetcorn medley

INGREDIENTS	METRIC	IMP.	U.S.
Boned loin of pork	1 kg	2 lb	2 lb
2 tbspn oil			
Garlic salt and pepper			
2 large carrots			
Cooked sweetcorn kernels	225 g	8 oz	½ lb
Cooked peas	225 g	8 oz	½ lb
1 tbspn flour			

Remove the skin and excess fat from the pork. Place these in a roasting tin in a moderately hot oven (375°F, 190°C, Gas Mark 5) to render out the dripping. Tie the joint neatly in shape with string. Brush the fat surface with oil and sprinkle with garlic salt and pepper. Push the pieces of pork fat to one side in the roasting tin, put in the joint and roast, basting occasionally with the pan juices, for 1½ hours, or until cooked through. Meanwhile, slice the carrots and cook in boiling salted water just to cover, until tender. Add the other vegetables and heat through. Drain, reserving the stock. Place the joint in a warm serving dish and surround with the vegetable medley. Keep hot. Strain the fat from the roasting tin into a pan, stir in the flour and cook, stirring, until browned. Gradually add the reserved vegetable stock and bring to the boil, stirring constantly, until the gravy is smooth and thickened. Add a little more water if necessary and season to taste. Serve separately in a gravy boat. Serves 6.

Blackcurrant soufflé

INGREDIENTS	METRIC	IMP.	U.S.
Unflavoured gelatine [gelatin]	15 g	½ oz	1 tbspn
3 tbspn cold water			
4 egg yolks			
Castor [granulated] sugar	50 g	2 oz	¼ cup
Sweetened blackcurrant purée	300 ml	½ pint	1¼ cups
Double [whipping] cream	150 ml	¼ pint	⅔ cup
4 egg whites			
DECORATION			
Chopped toasted almonds			
Whipped cream			

First prepare a 7 inch/18 cm soufflé dish by tying a band of double thickness greaseproof paper around the outside to come about 2 inches/5 cm above the top of the dish. Put the gelatine and cold water in a small pan and place over low heat until the gelatine has dissolved. Cool. Place the egg yolks and castor sugar in a bowl and whisk over hot water until the mixture is thick and light in colour. Remove from the heat and continue to whisk the mixture until it is cool. (If using a mixer it is not necessary to whisk over hot water.) Blend in the purée, then stir in the dissolved gelatine. Finally, fold in the lightly whipped cream and stiffly whisked egg whites. Pour into the prepared dish and leave to set in the refrigerator. To serve, carefully remove the band of paper and press chopped almonds into the sides of the soufflé. Decorate with whipped cream. Serves 6.

MENU 18

Southern fried chicken on saffron rice
Fried aubergines
Raspberry mousse
Apple and grape platter

Southern fried chicken on saffron rice

INGREDIENTS	METRIC	IMP.	U.S.
Long grain rice	225 g	8 oz	1⅓ cups
1 large pinch ground saffron			
4 southern fried chicken portions, defrosted			
Oil for frying			
SAUCE			
Butter	50 g	2 oz	¼ cup
1 onion, chopped			
Flour	40 g	1½ oz	6 tbspn
Canned tomatoes	425 g	15 oz	2 cups
1 tspn sugar			
1 tspn dried oregano			
1 bay leaf			
Salt and pepper			
2 tbspn double [whipping] cream			
1 tbspn chopped parsley and 1 chopped spring [green] onion to garnish			

First make the sauce. Melt the butter and use to sauté the onion gently until soft but not coloured. Remove from the heat and stir in the flour. Replace over heat and gradually add the tomatoes, sugar, oregano, bay leaf, and seasoning. Bring to the boil, stirring constantly, and simmer for 5 minutes. Press through a sieve and stir in the cream. Meanwhile cook the rice in plenty of boiling salted water with the saffron added. Rinse with hot water, drain and add seasoning. At the same time, deep fry the chicken portions as directed. Place a bed of saffron rice on a hot serving dish and arrange the chicken portions on top. Reheat the sauce if necessary but do not allow to boil. Spoon sauce over the chicken and garnish with parsley and onion. Serve with fried aubergines.

Raspberry mousse

INGREDIENTS	METRIC	IMP.	U.S.
Raspberry purée	600 ml	1 pint	2½ cups
Cream cheese	50 g	2 oz	¼ cup
3 tbspn castor [granulated] sugar			
Unflavoured gelatine [gelatin]	15 g	½ oz	1 tbspn
Cold water	4 tbspn	4 tbspn	⅓ cup
Double [whipping] cream	150 ml	¼ pint	⅔ cup
2 egg whites			
DECORATION			
Double [whipping] cream	150 ml	¼ pint	⅔ cup
Fresh or frozen raspberries			

Mix together the raspberry purée, cream cheese and castor sugar. Put the gelatine and water in a small pan and place over low heat until the gelatine has dissolved. Remove from the heat and allow to cool. Gradually add the dissolved gelatine to the raspberry mixture, whisking to combine the ingredients. Leave the mixture aside until it is beginning to set, then fold in the lightly whipped cream and stiffly beaten egg whites. Turn into a large dish or six individual dishes and chill in the refrigerator until firm. Before serving, pipe a decoration of whipped cream and top with the raspberries.
Note: Other fruit purées - strawberry, apricot or blackcurrant - may be used in place of the raspberry purée.

Fried aubergines

INGREDIENTS	METRIC	IMP.	U.S.
4 medium aubergines [eggplants]			
Salt and ground black pepper			
2 tbspn oil			

Cut the aubergines in half lengthwise, make several $\frac{1}{2}$ inch/1 cm deep slashes in each side, sprinkle cut surfaces with salt. Allow to stand for 30 minutes then dry with absorbent kitchen paper. Sprinkle with black pepper. Heat the oil and use to fry the aubergine halves gently for about 8 minutes, turning until golden brown.

Smoked fish cream
Strasbourg style goose
Parslied boiled potatoes
Exotic fruit salad

Smoked fish cream

INGREDIENTS	METRIC	IMP.	U.S.
Milk	300 ml	½ pint	1¼ cups
Thick smoked cod fillet	350 g	12 oz	¾ lb
Butter	25 g	1 oz	2 tbspn
Flour	20 g	¾ oz	3 tbspn
1 egg, separated			
½ tspn French mustard			
White pepper			
4 tbspn double [whipping] cream			
12 stuffed olives			
Liquid aspic	300 ml	½ pint	1½ cups

Place the milk in a saucepan and use to poach the cod very gently for about 15 minutes, until tender. If necessary add 2 or 3 tablespoons of water. Remove fish from liquid and flake, discarding skin and bones. Strain the liquid from cooking the fish and make up to 6 fl oz/200 ml/¾ cup if necessary with more milk. Melt the butter in a clean saucepan, stir in the flour and cook for 1 minute. Gradually add the measured liquid and bring to the boil, stirring constantly, until sauce is thick and smooth. Continue cooking for 2 minutes then beat in the egg yolk and remove from the heat. Taste and add mustard and white pepper. Pound up the fish and gradually add the sauce, or liquidise fish and sauce together in a blender. Place the mixture in a basin and stir in the cream. Beat the egg white until stiff, carefully fold into the mixture; use to fill a pie dish two-thirds full. Slice each stuffed olive into 4 and arrange the slices over the fish cream to cover as far as possible the surface of the mixture. Make up the aspic and chill until syrupy. Spoon over the cream and leave to set. Serves 6-8.

Strasbourg style goose

INGREDIENTS	METRIC	IMP.	U.S.
1 young goose	4 kg	8 lb	8 lb
2 large onions			
3 cooking [baking] apples			
4 tbspn soft [light] brown sugar			
3 tspn caraway seeds			
Salt and black pepper			
Sauerkraut	1 kg	2 lb	2 lb
6 tbspn beer			

Cook the goose giblets in sufficient salted water to cover until tender. Strain off stock and reserve. Chop the onions. Peel, core and dice the apples. Cook the onion and apple for 3 minutes in the stock, add the diced liver, brown sugar, caraway seeds, pepper and sauerkraut. Season the carcass with salt and pepper, stuff with the sauerkraut mixture. Prick the goose lightly with a fork, place on a trivet in a roasting pan. Put in a moderately hot oven (400°F, 200°C, Gas Mark 6) and roast for about 2½ hours. (Allow 20 minutes per 450 g/lb plus 20 minutes.) Baste occasionally with the beer and remove excess fat from roasting pan. Serves 6-8.

Exotic fruit salad

INGREDIENTS	METRIC	IMP.	U.S.
4 fresh figs			
2 Chinese gooseberries [Kiwi fruits]			
Green grapes	225 g	8 oz	½ lb
2 crisp apples			
2 pears			
2 tbspn lemon juice			
1 pomegranate			
2 tangerines			
Bottle dry cider	1 litre	35.2 fl oz	4½ cups

Slice the figs; peel and slice the Chinese gooseberries. Peel and remove the seeds from the green grapes. Slice the apples, leaving the peel on. Peel and slice the pears. Sprinkle the lemon juice on the apples and pears to prevent discolouring. Cut the pomegranate into small pieces. Peel and segment the tangerines, removing the seeds. Combine the prepared fruits and cover with the dry cider. Chill until serving time. Serves 6-8.

MENU 20

Jerusalem soup
Turkey with claret sauce
Roast parsnips and Brussels sprouts
Toasted apple pudding with brandied cream

Jerusalem soup

INGREDIENTS	METRIC	IMP.	U.S.
Jerusalem artichokes	450 g	1 lb	1 lb
1 medium onion			
Butter or margarine	25 g	1 oz	2 tbspn
2 tbspn flour			
Canned tomatoes	227 g	8 oz	1 cup
Chicken stock [broth]	600 ml	1 pint	2½ cups
1 strip of orange rind			
Pinch ground mace			
Salt and Pepper			
Orange juice	50 ml	2 fl oz	¼ cup
Grated orange rind			

Peel and slice the artichokes and onion. Sauté the sliced artichokes and onion in the butter until softened. Stir in the flour. Add the tomatoes, chicken stock, orange rind and seasonings. Cover and simmer for 15 minutes. Remove the orange rind. Liquidise the soup in a blender or sieve. Pour into a clean saucepan. Add the orange juice and reheat gently. Garnish with the grated orange rind. Serves 6.

Turkey with claret sauce

INGREDIENTS	METRIC	IMP.	U.S.
2 stalks celery			
Butter	75 g	3 oz	6 tbspn
Diced bacon	50 g	2 oz	⅓ cup
1 bottle Claret [dry red wine]			
Soft white breadcrumbs	175 g	6 oz	2 cups
Chopped walnuts	50 g	2 oz	½ cup
Salt and pepper			
1 beaten egg			
1 turkey	3–4 kg	6–8 lb	6–8 lb
Little oil			
1 chicken stock [bouillon] cube			
Flour	20 g	¾ oz	3 tbspn

Chop the celery finely and fry lightly in 2 oz/50 g of the butter with the bacon until the celery is soft but not coloured. Add ¼ pint/150 ml of the wine and boil rapidly to reduce by half. Stir in the breadcrumbs, walnuts and seasoning to taste. Bind with the lightly beaten egg and sufficient water to make a good firm stuffing consistency. Use to stuff the neck cavity of the turkey. Brush the bird lightly with oil, sprinkle with salt and pepper and place in a large roasting bag. Put the bag in a roasting tin in a moderately hot oven (375°F, 190°C, Gas Mark 5) for 2½-3 hours, depending on weight. Strain the clear stock from the bag into a measuring jug, add the stock cube and make up to ¾ pint/450 ml with more of the wine. Make a brown roux with the remaining butter and the flour. Gradually stir in the wine stock and cook, stirring constantly, until thick and smooth. Season to taste, serve separately. Serves 6.

Toasted apple pudding with brandied cream

INGREDIENTS	METRIC	IMP.	U.S.
4 slices white bread			
2 eggs			
Castor [granulated] sugar	100 g	4 oz	½ cup
1 tspn ground cinnamon			
¼ tspn salt			
1 tspn vanilla essence [extract]			
Milk	300 ml	½ pint	1¼ cups
Apple purée [applesauce]	225 g	8 oz	1 cup
Melted butter or margarine	25 g	1 oz	2 tbspn
1 egg white			
1 tbspn clear honey			
Double [whipping] cream	150 ml	¼ pint	⅔ cup
2 tbspn brandy			

Toast the bread lightly. Cut into ½ inch/1 cm strips. Beat the eggs lightly; stir in the sugar, cinnamon, salt, vanilla, milk, apple purée and butter. Place one-third of the toasted bread strips in a baking dish. Cover with half of the apple mixture. Repeat another layer of bread strips and remaining apple mixture. Top with remaining bread strips, making a lattice pattern. Bake in a moderate oven (325°F, 170°C, Gas Mark 3) for one hour or until the centre is set. Meanwhile to make the brandied cream, whisk the egg white until stiff. Gradually whisk the honey into the egg white. Whip the double cream and fold into the beaten egg white. Stir in the brandy. Serve the pudding warm with the sauce. Serves 6.

MENU
21

Chilled grapefruit halves
Baked hare with cranberries and chestnuts
Oven-baked potatoes and braised celery
Raisin lattice pie

Baked hare with cranberries and chestnuts

INGREDIENTS	METRIC	IMP.	U.S.
1 jointed hare			
Seasoned flour	75 g	3 oz	¾ cup
2 tbspn oil			
Butter	50 g	2 oz	¼ cup
2 large onions, sliced			
Beef stock [broth]	450 ml	¾ pint	1¾ cups
4 tbspn Marsala			
Chestnuts	450 g	1 lb	1 lb
Cranberries	225 g	8 oz	½ lb
Salt and pepper			

Coat the hare joints and liver in the seasoned flour and brown all over in the hot oil and butter. Transfer joints to an ovenproof casserole, and add the sliced onion, stock and Marsala. Pour over the pan juices from browning the hare. Cover and cook in a moderate oven (325°F, 170°C, Gas Mark 3) for 2 hours. Meanwhile, boil the chestnuts for 15-20 minutes, or until the shell and skin can easily be removed. Add to the casserole with the cranberries, sprinkle in any remaining seasoned flour and stir gently. Cover and return to the oven for a further 20 minutes. Adjust the seasoning.

Raisin lattice pie

INGREDIENTS	METRIC	IMP.	U.S.
Plain [all-purpose] flour	225 g	8 oz	2 cups
½ tspn salt			
Whipped white cooking fat [shortening]	100 g	4 oz	½ cup
2 tbspn water			
1 egg white			
FILLING			
2 medium oranges			
Cornflour [cornstarch]	25 g	1 oz	2 tbspn
Seedless [dark seedless] raisins	225 g	8 oz	1½ cups
Brown sugar	50 g	2 oz	¼ cup
Butter	50 g	2 oz	¼ cup

Sieve the flour and salt into a bowl. Add the fat and water and mix with a fork until a ball of dough is formed. Knead lightly. Line a 9 inch/22 cm sandwich tin with three quarters of the pastry and roll the remainder into six ½ inch/1 cm strips. Dampen pastry edges with egg white. Grate the rind from the oranges and squeeze the juice. Make juice up to ½ pint/300 ml/1¼ cups with water. Blend the cornflour with 2 table-spoons of the liquid. Boil the remainder with the raisins and sugar. Add the moistened cornflour and bring to the boil, stirring constantly. Add the butter and orange rind, cool and pour into the prepared pastry case. Place the pastry strips in a lattice pattern over the filling. Brush with egg white and bake in a moderately hot oven (400°F, 200°C, Gas Mark 6) for 30 minutes. Serve hot or cold.

Hot consommé
Colonial goose
Roast potatoes, onion rings and carrots
Apple and chestnut charlotte

Colonial goose

INGREDIENTS	METRIC	IMP.	U.S.
Leg of lamb	2.2 kg	4½ lb	4½ lb
Dried apricots	100 g	4 oz	¾ cup —
Fresh white breadcrumbs	100 g	4 oz	1¼ cups
Butter	25 g	1 oz	2 tbspn
1 tbspn clear honey			
Grated [minced] onion	50 g	2 oz	¼ cup
¼ tspn dried thyme			
¼ tspn salt			
Pinch freshly ground black pepper			
1 egg			

Lay the meat, fat side down, on a wooden board. With a small, sharp pointed knife, work the meat away from the bone, from the top of the leg down to the first joint. Now, cut along the line of the bone from the opposite end of the leg. Work the flesh away from the bone, being careful not to puncture the skin in any other place. Sever the bone from all the flesh and ligaments and draw out the bone. With a pair of scissors, snip the apricots in two. Place the breadcrumbs in a basin and stir in the apricots. Turn butter into a small saucepan and add honey. Stir over low heat until melted then stir in the onion. Add to the breadcrumb mixture, with the herbs and seasoning. Whisk the egg lightly, pour into stuffing ingredients and beat until well blended. Stuff the leg and weigh it. Roast in a moderate oven (350°F, 180°C, Gas Mark 4) for 30 minutes per lb/450 g. Serves 8.

Apple and chestnut charlotte

INGREDIENTS	METRIC	IMP.	U.S.
26 boudoir biscuits [ladyfingers]			
4 tbspn dry sherry			
Chestnut purée	150 ml	¼ pint	⅔ cup
Apple purée [applesauce]	300 ml	½ pint	1¼ cups
Double [whipping] cream	300 ml	½ pint	1¼ cups
Marrons glacés for decoration			

Dip 2 boudoir biscuits in the sherry and place in the bottom of a Tupperware Jel 'n' serve. Dip 16 more biscuits and arrange in the mould filling the curves. Mix together the chestnut purée and the apple purée and put half into the mould. Then add half the whipped cream and top with four biscuits. Add remaining purée and cream (reserving a little for decoration) and finish with a layer of biscuits. Seal the mould and press firmly. Chill. To serve remove seal and turn the charlotte on to a serving dish. Remove the design seal and lift off the mould. Decorate with the reserved cream and marrons glacés. An 8 inch/20 cm spring-sided or loose-bottomed mould could be substituted, spacing out the biscuits evenly. Serves 8.

Avocado starters

Gingered autumn chicken

Pasta shells

Plum fritters

Red wine sauce

Avocado starters

INGREDIENTS	METRIC	IMP.	U.S.
2 avocado pears			
1 canned red pimiento			
1 large carrot			
Webb's [small Bibb] lettuce	100 g	4 oz	½
8 canned anchovy fillets			
2 tbspn mayonnaise			

Cut the avocados in half and remove the stones. Slice the pimiento finely, coarsely grate the carrot and shred the lettuce. Reserve 4 anchovy fillets and 4 pieces of red pimiento for the garnish. Chop the remaining anchovy fillets roughly, toss together with the sliced pimiento, the carrot, lettuce and mayonnaise. Divide the filling between the four portions, topping each one with an anchovy fillet rolled round a piece of pimiento. If liked, serve with lettuce leaves as the stuffed avocado is rather rich.

Gingered Autumn chicken

INGREDIENTS	METRIC	IMP.	U.S.
4 chicken portions			
Flour for coating			
2 tbspn oil			
1 large onion, chopped			
1 chicken stock [bouillon] cube			
3 pieces stem ginger, chopped			
½ tspn ground ginger			
2 bay leaves			
2 medium Conference [cooking] pears			
2 medium eating apples			
Plums	225 g	8 oz	½ lb
2 tbspn ginger syrup			
Lemon juice to taste			
Salt and pepper			
1 tbspn chopped parsley			

Divide the chicken portions into serving-size pieces and coat with flour. Heat the oil in a flameproof casserole and use to fry the chicken pieces until crisp and golden brown all over. Remove chicken from the pan. Add the onion to the remaining fat and fry gently until just turning colour. Return the chicken pieces to the pan. Make up the stock cube with ¾ pint/400 ml/scant 2 cups boiling water and stir in the chopped ginger, and the ground ginger, and pour over the chicken. Bring to the boil, add bay leaves, cover and simmer gently for 20 minutes. Peel, core and slice the pears and apples. Halve and stone the plums. Add the fruit and ginger syrup to the casserole. Cover and simmer gently until the chicken is tender. Add lemon juice to taste and adjust seasoning. Serve garnished with chopped parsley.

Autumn fruits such as plums and damsons have a brief season. Use them in savoury dishes, sweets and sauces. A delicious sauce that keeps well is made by stewing the fruit in cider vinegar with spices and sugar. Sieve to remove stones, boil again for a few minutes to make the sauce really thick and bottle. Stored in the refrigerator, covered, it keeps for weeks. A savoury sauce to use at once can be made by cooking 6 large stoned plums in a very little water with a knob of butter, 1 tablespoon sugar and a pinch of ground cinnamon or allspice. Cook until soft, then sieve to make a smooth purée.

Plum fritters

INGREDIENTS	METRIC	IMP.	U.S.
Large fairly ripe plums [prune-plums]	700 g	1½ lb	1½ lb
Roughly chopped hazelnuts	50 g	2 oz	½ cup
Castor [granulated] sugar	25 g	1 oz	2 tbspn
BATTER			
Flour	200 g	7 oz	1¾ cups
Castor [granulated] sugar	25 g	1 oz	2 tbspn
Milk	175 ml	6 fl oz	¾ cup
2 tbspn brandy			
1 tbspn oil			
3 eggs, separated			
Oil for frying			
Castor [granulated] sugar to sprinkle			

First make the batter. Sieve the flour into a bowl and stir in the sugar. Gradually beat in the milk, then the brandy, corn oil and finally the egg yolks. Allow to stand in a cool place while you prepare the plums. Choose plums which are just ripe enough to slit open at one side and extract the stone. Mix together the nuts and sugar and use to fill the cavity in each plum, pressing together again into shape. Beat the egg whites until stiff and fold into the batter. Coat each filled plum with the batter and fry in deep hot oil until rich golden brown. Drain and sprinkle liberally with castor sugar. Serve with Red wine sauce.

Red wine sauce

INGREDIENTS	METRIC	IMP.	U.S.
Red wine	175 ml	6 fl oz	¾ cup
Red fruit juice or orange juice	175 ml	6 fl oz	¾ cup
Sugar	50 g	2 oz	¼ cup
Pinch ground cinnamon			
1 clove			
1 tspn cornflour [cornstarch]			

Place the wine in a saucepan with the fruit juice, sugar, cinnamon and clove. Bring to boiling point. Moisten the cornflour with a little cold water, add to the pan and bring to the boil again, stirring constantly, until the sauce is thickened and clear. Remove the clove.

MENU
24

Apple and avocado salad
Chicken curry Veronique
Fluffy boiled rice
Saucy lemon pudding and cream

Apple and avocado salad

INGREDIENTS	METRIC	IMP.	U.S.
2 avocado pears			
2 dessert apples			
1 bunch watercress			
Salted peanuts	50 g	2 oz	½ cup
LEMON DRESSING			
Olive oil	6 tbspn	6 tbspn	½ cup
2 tbspn lemon juice			
Salt and pepper			
1 tspn mild Continental mustard			
1 clove garlic, crushed			
1 tspn castor [granulated] sugar			

Cut the avocados in half, discard the stones and remove the flesh without damaging the skins. Chop the flesh roughly. Core the apples and chop roughly. Reserve 4 sprigs of watercress for the garnish and chop the remainder. Chop the peanuts. Mix together all ingredients for the dressing and beat really well. Lightly toss the chopped avocado, apple, watercress and nuts in the dressing and pile back into the avocado shells. Garnish with watercress.

Chicken curry Veronique

INGREDIENTS	METRIC	IMP.	U.S.
2 medium onions			
4 chicken portions			
Butter	50 g	2 oz	$\frac{1}{4}$ cup
1 tbspn oil			
2 tbspn curry powder			
Chicken stock [broth]	450 ml	$\frac{3}{4}$ pint	2 cups
2 grated carrots			
2 tbspn flour			
Evaporated milk	156 ml	$5\frac{1}{2}$ fl oz	$\frac{2}{3}$ cup
Green grapes, halved and deseeded	225 g	8 oz	$\frac{1}{2}$ lb

Finely chop the onions and fry gently with the chicken in the butter and oil until golden brown. Add the curry powder and cook for 10-15 minutes, stirring occasionally, until the chicken pieces are brown on all sides. Gradually add the stock, stirring constantly. Bring to the boil and add the carrot. Cover and simmer for 1 hour, stirring occasionally. Remove the curry from heat; whisk the flour into the evaporated milk made up to $\frac{1}{2}$ pint/300 ml with cold water and stir quickly into the curry. Add the grapes, return to the heat and bring back to the boil. Simmer for a further 10 minutes. Serve with fluffy boiled rice.

Saucy lemon pudding

INGREDIENTS	METRIC	IMP.	U.S.
3 eggs			
Castor [granulated] sugar	225 g	8 oz	1 cup
$\frac{1}{4}$ tspn salt			
Lemon juice	50 ml	2 fl oz	$\frac{1}{4}$ cup
Grated rind of 1 lemon			
Plain [all-purpose] flour	25 g	1 oz	$\frac{1}{4}$ cup
Milk	350 ml	12 fl oz	$1\frac{1}{2}$ cups
Melted Butter	40 g	$1\frac{1}{2}$ oz	3 tbspn

Separate the eggs and whisk the egg whites until frothy. Gradually whisk in half of the sugar until soft peaks form. Beat the egg yolks with the remaining sugar and the salt. Stir in the lemon juice, rind, flour, milk and the melted butter until well combined. Fold gently into the egg white meringue. Turn into a lightly buttered 2 pint/generous 1 litre/5 cup baking dish. Set the dish in a pan of hot water. Bake in a moderate oven (350°F, 180°C, Gas Mark 4) for 50 minutes or until lightly browned on top. Serve warm with cream.

Cream of chestnut soup
Pigeon with orange sauce
Red cabbage and carrot layer
Chocolate cups with ginger cream

Cream of chestnut soup

INGREDIENTS	METRIC	IMP.	U.S.
Chestnuts	450 g	1 lb	1 lb
1 small onion			
2 stalks celery			
Butter	25 g	1 oz	2 tbspn
1 tbspn flour			
Milk	450 ml	$\frac{3}{4}$ pint	2 cups
Water	300 ml	$\frac{1}{2}$ pint	$1\frac{1}{4}$ cups
Salt and pepper			
Fried bread croûtons			

Boil the chestnuts for 15-20 minutes. Shell and skin them. Cook in enough water to cover for 30 minutes, until they are tender. Strain, then sieve or liquidise the cooked chestnuts in a blender. Chop the onion and celery finely. Sauté in the butter until soft. Stir in the flour and cook for 2-3 minutes. Slowly add the milk, water and chestnut purée. Simmer gently for 15 minutes. Season to taste with salt and pepper and serve with croûtons.

Red cabbage and carrot layer

INGREDIENTS	METRIC	IMP.	U.S.
1 thick slice fat bacon			
1 small red cabbage, shredded			
Carrots, cut in thin strips	225 g	8 oz	$\frac{1}{2}$ lb
Salt and pepper			
Orange juice	150 ml	$\frac{1}{4}$ pint	$\frac{1}{2}$ cup
Butter	15 g	$\frac{1}{2}$ oz	1 tbspn

Place the bacon in the bottom of a flameproof casserole, add the cabbage and julienne strips of carrot, sprinkling the layers with salt and pepper. Pour in the orange juice, arrange dots of butter on top, cover and cook over moderate heat for 20 minutes.

Pigeon is full of flavour but it needs careful cooking or it may be tough. Other good ways to cook pigeon are as follows: Remove the plump breast meat from each side of the breastbone, brush with soy sauce, season and wrap in foil. Roast in a moderately hot oven for 45 minutes or until the flesh is tender. Or put a little butter in a flameproof casserole, cook the pigeons in it until sealed on all sides, then season, and add a few tablespoons of strong chicken stock. Cover tightly and simmer for about 1 hour or until tender. The flesh is actually steamed, so make sure the lid of the pan is a good fit, so it does not boil dry.

Pigeon with orange sauce

INGREDIENTS	METRIC	IMP.	U.S.
3 tbspn oil			
4 pigeons			
1 onion			
1 tbspn redcurrant jelly			
Chicken stock [broth]	150 ml	¼ pint	½ cup
Orange juice	150 ml	¼ pint	½ cup
Salt and pepper			
2 tspn cornflour [cornstarch]			
Few orange slices and sprigs of watercress to garnish			

Heat the oil in a frying pan and fry the pigeons until golden brown. Remove and put into a casserole. Finely chop the onion, add to the frying pan and cook gently until soft. Stir in the jelly, stock, orange juice and salt and pepper to taste. Stir well and pour over the pigeons. Cover casserole with a tight fitting lid and cook in a moderate oven (325°F, 170°C, Gas Mark 3) for 2 hours. Remove pigeons, place on a hot serving dish and keep warm. Strain the pan juices into a saucepan and stir in the cornflour moistened with 2 tablespoons cold water. Bring to the boil, stirring constantly, and cook until sauce is thickened and smooth. Garnish the pigeons with slices of fresh orange and watercress and hand the sauce separately.

Chocolate cups with ginger cream

INGREDIENTS	METRIC	IMP.	U.S.
Plain [dark] chocolate	225 g	8 oz	½ lb
4 pieces stem ginger			
1 tbspn ginger syrup			
Double [whipping] cream	150 ml	¼ pint	½ cup
Chopped pistachio nuts to decorate			

Melt the chocolate in a basin over a pan of hot water. Using the back of a teaspoon, coat the insides of paper bun cases with a layer of melted chocolate then chill until set. Repeat twice until the cases are evenly coated. Remove the paper cases. Chop three pieces of ginger, mix with the ginger syrup and divide between the chocolate cups. Whip the cream until thick and place in a piping bag fitted with a star nozzle. Pipe a rosette of cream into each chocolate cup and sprinkle lightly with chopped pistachio nuts. Slice the remaining piece of ginger and use to decorate rosettes. Chill for up to 2 hours and serve immediately on removing from the refrigerator.

MENU

26

Cauliflower and bacon ramekins
Game pie
Sovereign salad
Grapefruit Alaska

Cauliflower and bacon ramekins

INGREDIENTS	METRIC	IMP.	U.S.
1 small cauliflower			
Milk	150 ml	$\frac{1}{4}$ pint	$\frac{1}{2}$ cup
Butter	20 g	$\frac{3}{4}$ oz	$1\frac{1}{2}$ tbspn
Flour	15 g	$\frac{1}{2}$ oz	2 tbspn
Salt and pepper			
$\frac{1}{4}$ tspn grated nutmeg			
4 tbspn cooked macaroni			
Streaky [side] bacon	50 g	2 oz	2 slices
2 tbspn single cream [half & half]			
Grated Cheddar cheese	50 g	2 oz	$\frac{1}{2}$ cup

Break the cauliflower into florets and cook in boiling salted water for about 10 minutes, or until just tender. Drain, and use the water to make the milk up to 8 fl oz/225 ml. Melt the butter, stir in the flour, cook for 1 minute, add the milk liquid, salt, pepper and nutmeg and cook, stirring constantly, over a moderate heat until smooth and thick. Divide the cooked macaroni between four greased individual oven-proof casseroles. Derind the bacon, dice finely, and fry lightly. Mix the bacon bits with the cauliflower florets and place on top of the macaroni. Pour over the sauce, then a little cream and finally sprinkle with grated cheese. Place under a hot grill until the surface is crisp and golden.

Game pie

INGREDIENTS	METRIC	IMP.	U.S.
2 cooked grouse			
Cooked pheasant or rabbit	225 g	8 oz	1 cup
Red wine	300 ml	½ pint	1¼ cups
Salt and ground black pepper			
1 bay leaf			
Chopped bacon	50 g	2 oz	¼ cup
Lambs' liver	100 g	4 oz	¼ lb
Sliced mushrooms	100 g	4 oz	1 cup
Puff pastry [paste]	350 g	12 oz	¾ lb
Beaten egg to glaze			

Remove the meat from the grouse, cut it quite coarsely and place in a bowl with the pheasant or rabbit, also cut quite coarsely. Pour over the red wine, add some seasoning and a bay leaf. Cover and leave in the refrigerator to marinate, preferably overnight, or for at least 4 hours. Place the bacon in a pan and heat to allow the fat to run. Add the liver, cut in small pieces, and brown lightly on all sides, transfer to a pie dish. Discard the bay leaf from the marinade and mix the game and marinade with the bacon and liver in the pie dish. Sprinkle over the mushrooms and add more seasoning. Add more wine if necessary to come halfway up the dish. Roll out the pastry thinly and use to cover the dish. Flake and flute the pastry edges and make a hole in the centre for the steam to escape. Make some pastry leaves for decoration from the pastry trimmings. Brush with beaten egg and bake in a hot oven (425°F, 220°C, Gas Mark 7) for 20 minutes. Reduce the heat to moderate (350°F, 180°C, Gas Mark 4) and bake for a further 40 minutes, covering the pastry with foil to prevent it over-browning.

Sovereign salad

INGREDIENTS	METRIC	IMP.	U.S.
Red cabbage	450 g	1 lb	1 lb
1 green-skinned eating apple			
1 celery heart			
4 sprigs watercress			
DRESSING			
½ tspn salt and ¼ tspn pepper			
½ tspn dry mustard			
Pinch castor [granulated] sugar			
1 tbspn lemon juice			
2 tbspn oil			

Shred the cabbage finely into a bowl, discarding the core and thick stems. Core and slice the apple thinly. Slice the celery heart finely, and chop up the watercress, reserving 4 tiny top sprigs for the garnish. To make the dressing, stir the seasonings and sugar into the lemon juice and gradually beat in the oil. Toss the apple, celery and chopped watercress in the dressing until well coated. Divide the shredded cabbage between four individual salad bowls, cover with the celery mixture and dressing and top with the reserved sprigs of watercress.

Grapefruit Alaska

INGREDIENTS	METRIC	IMP.	U.S.
2 fresh grapefruit			
2 tbspn sweet sherry			
3 egg whites			
Castor [granulated] sugar	75 g	3 oz	⅓ cup
½ tspn vanilla essence [extract]			
4 scoops vanilla ice cream			

Cut the grapefruit in half, separate the segments and sprinkle with the sherry. Whisk the egg whites until soft peaks form. Gradually add the sugar, whisking until very stiff peaks form. Add the vanilla essence. At serving time, top each grapefruit half with a scoop of ice cream. Cover the ice cream with the meringue, sealing the ice cream with the meringue to the edge of the grapefruit. Place on a baking sheet in a very hot oven (475°F, 240°C, Gas Mark 9) for 3 minutes. Serve immediately.

MENU 27

Tomato juice cocktail
Roast pheasant
Frosted Brussels sprouts with croûtons
Fresh lime mousse
Devils on horseback

Roast pheasant

INGREDIENTS	METRIC	IMP.	U.S.
1 plump pheasant			
Salt and pepper			
Butter	25 g	1 oz	2 tbspn
Large slice fat [side] bacon			
Red wine	150 ml	¼ pint	½ cup
Little flour			
2 slices white bread			
Liver pâté	50 g	2 oz	2 oz

> **Tomato juice** can be flavoured in several ways to make delicious cocktails for meal starters. Try stirring ½ teaspoon lemon juice, 1 teaspoon orange juice, a pinch of salt and a sprinkle of black pepper into every glass. Or add ½ teaspoon Worcestershire sauce and 1 teaspoon each of very finely chopped parsley and chives to every glass.

Season the bird inside and out with salt and pepper. Put half the butter inside the carcass, and cover the breast with the bacon. Stand on a trivet in a roasting tin. Melt the remaining butter and pour over the bird. Roast in a hot oven (450°F, 230°C, Gas Mark 8) for 10 minutes. Pour the wine over the bird, baste well, reduce heat to moderately hot (400°F, 200°C, Gas Mark 6) and return to the oven for a further 30 minutes, basting once during this time. Take the tin from the oven, remove bacon rasher, baste with the juices, dredge lightly with flour and baste again. Raise oven heat to hot (450°F, 230°C, Gas Mark 8) return the tin and continue roasting for a further 10 minutes. Trim crusts from bread and fry or toast then spread with the pâté. Serve the pheasant on this, surrounded by game chips and Brussels sprouts.
Note: Ask the poulterer for three tail feathers. Cut to an even length and arrange at the tail end to disguise the legs.

Frosted Brussels sprouts with croûtons

INGREDIENTS	METRIC	IMP.	U.S.
Brussels sprouts	450 g	1 lb	1 lb
Butter	15 g	½ oz	1 tbspn
2 tbspn finely chopped onion			
1 tbspn flour			
2 tspn brown sugar			
½ tspn salt			
½ tspn dry mustard			
Milk	125 ml	4 fl oz	½ cup
Soured cream	150 ml	¼ pint	⅔ cup
Fried bread croûtons			

Trim the Brussels sprouts. Cook them in boiling salted water until tender. While the sprouts are cooking, melt the butter in a saucepan. Add the onion and cook until limp, but not brown. Stir in the flour, brown sugar, salt and dry mustard. Cook for 1 minute. Gradually add the milk and cook, stirring constantly, until the sauce thickens and boils. Remove from the heat. Stir in the soured cream. Drain the cooked Brussels sprouts. Pour the soured cream sauce over the sprouts. Reheat, but do not allow to boil. Garnish with croûtons.

Fresh lime mousse

INGREDIENTS	METRIC	IMP.	U.S.
1 packet lime jelly [3 oz package lime-flavoured gelatin]			
Hot water	300 ml	$\frac{1}{2}$ pint	$1\frac{1}{4}$ cups
Evaporated milk	450 g	$\frac{3}{4}$ pint	2 cups
Rind and juice of 2 fresh limes			
Double [whipping] cream	150 ml	$\frac{1}{4}$ pint	$\frac{1}{2}$ cup

Dissolve the jelly in the water and stir in the evaporated milk, lime rind and juice (set aside a little rind for decoration). Pour the mixture into a dampened mould and refrigerate until set. Turn out on to a plate. Whisk the cream until stiff and pipe around the jelly. Sprinkle with the lime rind.

Devils on horseback

INGREDIENTS	METRIC	IMP.	U.S.
2 tbspn French mustard			
Pinch cayenne pepper			
Few drops Tabasco sauce			
8 slices streaky [side] bacon			
16 shelled oysters			

Mix the mustard with the cayenne pepper and Tabasco sauce. Spread thinly on one side of the bacon slices. Cut each bacon rasher in half. Wrap each piece of bacon around an oyster with the mustard on the inside. Secure with a wooden pick or skewer. Grill for 10 minutes or until the bacon is crisp. Or, bake in a hot oven (450°F, 230°C, Gas Mark 8) for 10-15 minutes. Serve on buttered toast.

MENU 28

Golden pumpkin soup
Roast goose with apple and raisin stuffing
Floury boiled potatoes
Red cabbage
Damson cheesecake

Golden pumpkin soup

INGREDIENTS	METRIC	IMP.	U.S.
Pumpkin	1 kg	2 lb	2 lb
1 small onion, finely chopped			
2 tbspn chopped green pepper			
Butter or margarine	25 g	1 oz	2 tbspns
Milk	300 ml	$\frac{1}{2}$ pint	$1\frac{1}{4}$ cups
Chicken stock [broth]	300 ml	$\frac{1}{2}$ pint	$1\frac{1}{4}$ cups
1 tspn salt			
$\frac{1}{4}$ tspn pepper			
1 tbspn tomato purée [paste]			
Few drops Worcestershire sauce			
Chopped chives			

Peel and remove seeds from the pumpkin. Steam until tender: then mash or liquidise until smooth. Sauté the onion and green pepper in the butter until soft. Stir in the pumpkin purée and milk, stock, salt, pepper, tomato purée and Worcestershire sauce. Serve very hot, garnished with chopped chives. Serves 6.

Roast goose with apple and raisin stuffing

INGREDIENTS	METRIC	IMP.	U.S.
1 goose	4–5 kg	8–10 lb	8–10 lb
Seedless raisins	100 g	4 oz	¾ cup
1 medium onion			
6 medium cooking [baking] apples			
Butter	40 g	1½ oz	3 tbspn
Soft white breadcrumbs	150 g	5 oz	1⅔ cups
Chopped hazelnuts, walnuts or almonds	50 g	2 oz	½ cup
3 tbspn chopped parsley			
1 tspn dried marjoram			
Salt and pepper			
Finely grated rind of ½ lemon			
½ tspn ground mixed spices			
2 tbspn clear honey			
2 tbspn water			
Parsley sprigs to garnish			

Wash the goose and dry thoroughly with kitchen paper. Pour ½ pint/300 ml boiling water over the raisins and leave them for 20 minutes until plump and then drain. Finely chop the onion and peel, core and coarsely grate 3 of the apples. Heat the butter in a large heavy pan and cook the chopped onion over low heat until soft. Dice the goose liver and add to the onions with the raisins and grated apple. Cook for 2-3 minutes, stirring all the time until the liver is light brown. Turn into a mixing bowl and add the breadcrumbs, nuts, chopped parsley and marjoram. Mix well together and season with salt and pepper. Stuff the goose with the apple and raisin stuffing and secure with skewers. Truss the bird securely. Place the goose breast side up on a rack set in a large shallow roasting tin and roast in a moderate oven (325°F, 170°C, Gas Mark 3) for 3-3½ hours. or allow 20 minutes per lb/450 g. Pour away the fat as it collects and turn the goose halfway through cooking. Core and thickly slice the remaining apples and place in an ovenproof dish. Sprinkle with the lemon rind and mixed spices. Spoon over the honey and water. Cover the dish and place in the oven with the goose 45 minutes before the end of the cooking time. Remove the goose when ready to a heated serving dish, remove the string and skewers and garnish with the apple slices and parsley. Serves 6.

Damson cheesecake

INGREDIENTS	METRIC	IMP.	U.S.
Butter	100 g	4 oz	½ cup
Crushed digestive biscuits [Graham crackers]	225 g	8 oz	½ lb
Sugar	225 g	8 oz	1 cup
Damsons [damson plums]	225 g	8 oz	½ lb
Water	150 ml	¼ pint	⅔ cup
FILLING			
Cream cheese	450 g	1 lb	1 lb
4 eggs, separated			
Lemon juice	4 tbspn	4 tbspn	⅓ cup
Grated rind of ½ lemon			
1 tbspn gelatine [gelatin]			
Cold water	6 tbspn	6 tbspn	½ cup
5 tbspn sugar			
Double [whipping] cream	4 tbspn	4 tbspn	⅓ cup

Melt the butter and stir into the biscuit crumbs with 4 oz/100 g of the sugar. Press this to the base and sides of a greased loose-bottomed cake tin and place in a moderately hot oven (400°F, 200°C, Gas Mark 6) for 10 minutes. Cool. Halve and stone the damsons. Place the water and remaining sugar in a saucepan and allow sugar to dissolve over gentle heat. Use the syrup to poach the damsons gently for 20 minutes and cool in the syrup. Drain the damsons and arrange in the base of the flan case. To make the filling, soften the cream cheese and beat until smooth. Gradually beat in the egg yolks then the lemon juice and rind. Allow the gelatine to dissolve in the water in a basin over a pan of hot water then stir into the cheese mixture. Beat the egg whites stiffly and gradually beat in the sugar. Whip the cream. Fold the meringue and whipped cream into the cheese mixture alternately. Spoon the cheesecake mixture over the damsons, smooth the top and chill well. Dip tin in hot water, remove and serve the cheesecake on the metal base. Serves 6.

MENU

29

Grilled grapefruit
Creamed turkey duchesse
Decorated ice cream dessert
Gaelic coffee

Creamed turkey duchesse

INGREDIENTS	METRIC	IMP.	U.S.
Button mushrooms	175 g	6 oz	1½ cups
1 green pepper			
Chicken stock [broth]	150 ml	¼ pint	½ cup +
Béchamel [white] sauce	450 ml	¾ pint	2 cups
4 tbspn double [whipping] cream			
1 egg yolk			
Salt and pepper			
1½ tspn Tabasco			
Mashed potato	750 g	1½ lb	4 cups
2 eggs			
Little milk			
Cooked turkey	350 g	12 oz	¾ lb
Parsley to garnish			

Remove stalk ends from the mushrooms and keep to one side. Deseed the pepper and cut into chunks. Simmer the mushrooms and green pepper in a little chicken stock, until just tender, then drain and reserve liquid. Add the mushroom stalks to the chicken stock and reduce rapidly, to give approximately 2 tablespoons mushroom essence. Strain this into the sauce, together with the cream and one egg yolk. Beat well and season to taste with salt, pepper and Tabasco. Heat the sauce through for 2-3 minutes, but do not allow to boil. Beat the potato until smooth and add one egg and a little milk. Fork the duchesse potato into a decorative border around the edge of an ovenproof dish, and place in a moderately hot oven (400°F, 200°C, Gas Mark 6) for 8 minutes. Beat the remaining egg and use to glaze the potato lightly. Return to the oven until golden brown. Cut the turkey into small pieces and fold into the sauce with the vegetables. Heat through together. Pile turkey mixture into the potato ring and garnish with parsley. Serves 6.

Decorated ice cream dessert

INGREDIENTS	METRIC	IMP.	U.S.
Double [whipping] cream	150 ml	¼ pint	½ cup
2 tbspn rum			
Few orange segments			
Pack Rum and Raisin ice cream	½ litre	17 fl oz	1 pint
16 ratafia biscuits [cookies]			
Small strip angelica			

Whip the cream with the rum until stiff enough to pipe. Place in a piping bag with a small rose nozzle. Have ready a few orange segments or other seasonal fruit to decorate. Chill a flat glass serving dish, turn out the ice cream on to the plate and quickly pipe round the top and at both ends. Decorate with ratafia biscuits, fruit and leaves of angelica. Serve at once. Serves 6.
Note: **This sweet can be fully prepared and put uncovered into the freezer just before serving a meal so that it can be produced when required.**

Gaelic coffee Warm stemmed goblets, and put 1 teaspoon sugar in each glass. Add 1 tablespoon whiskey to each glass and stir well. Carefully pour in very hot black coffee to come two-thirds of the way up the glasses, stirring gently until the sugar dissolves. Top up each glass with half-whipped double cream, pouring it in over the back of a teaspoon so that it rests on the surface of the coffee without mingling.

Salmon pâté with olives
Turkey with chestnuts
Pastry fleurons
Braised fennel
Raspberry cracker meringue

Salmon pâté with olives

INGREDIENTS	METRIC	IMP.	U.S.
Butter	*15 g*	*½ oz*	*1 tbspn*
Flour	*15 g*	*½ oz*	*2 tbspn*
Milk	*300 ml*	*½ pint*	*1¼ cups*
1 tspn salt			
Freshly ground black pepper			
Cooked fresh salmon	*450 g*	*1 lb*	*1 lb*
1 small onion, chopped			
Finely grated rind and juice of 1 lemon			
Few drops Tabasco			
Unflavoured gelatine [gelatin]	*15 g*	*½ oz*	*1 tbspn*
18 stuffed green olives			
1 egg white			

Melt the butter in a saucepan and stir in the flour. Cook over low heat, stirring, for 2 minutes. Add the milk to the pan, season to taste and bring to the boil stirring constantly. Cover and leave to cool. Remove bones and skin from the salmon. Liquidise the sauce, onion, salmon, lemon rind and Tabasco in a blender, or pound well in a bowl. Dissolve the gelatine in the lemon juice and stir in the salmon mixture. Add 12 olives and fold in the stiffly beaten egg white. Pour into an ovenproof dish. Garnish with the remaining olives, sliced, cover and chill for at least 4 hours. Service with hot toast or French bread. Serves 8.

Turkey with chestnuts

INGREDIENTS	METRIC	IMP.	U.S.
Chestnuts	450 g	1 lb	1 lb
Pork [bulk pork] sausage-meat	350 g	12 oz	¾ lb
Salt and pepper			
1 turkey	3.5 kg	8 lb	8 lb
Large slice fat bacon			
2 small onions, quartered			
2 small carrots, quartered			
4 tbspn brandy			
4 tbspn port			
1 tspn cornflour [cornstarch]			
Fleurons to garnish			

Slit the skins of the chestnuts, place in a roasting tin in a hot oven for 10 minutes, or until the skins split. Peel and cook in boiling, salted water for 20 minutes, or until tender. Reserve a few whole chestnuts for the garnish. Chop and combine the rest of the chestnuts with the sausage-meat, season to taste and use to stuff the turkey at the neck end. Cover the turkey breast with the bacon and roast it for about 2½ hours, or until golden brown, removing the bacon for the last 30 minutes of cooking time. (See method on p. 79.)

Meanwhile, cook the giblets with the onion and carrot. To serve, pour the brandy over the turkey and ignite. Strain the stock from the giblets, add the port and use to make a sauce with the juices in the roasting tin. Reduce by half and thicken with the moistened cornflour. Reheat the chestnuts in the sauce. Serve the turkey surrounded with chestnuts and pastry fleurons.
Note: If the fleurons are made at home, cut crescent shapes with a round biscuit cutter from puff pastry, glaze with beaten egg and place in the hottest part of the oven to bake when you remove the bacon from the turkey breast. If necessary, raise the heat slightly to brown the turkey well and encourage the fleurons to rise. Serves 8.

Raspberry cracker meringue

INGREDIENTS	METRIC	IMP.	U.S.
Cream crackers [soda crackers]	8	8	22
3 egg whites			
Castor [granulated] sugar	175 g	6 oz	¾ cup
½ tspn baking powder			
Chopped walnuts	50 g	2 oz	½ cup
Double [whipping] cream	150 ml	¼ pint	½ cup
Castor [granulated] sugar	50 g	2 oz	¼ cup
½ tspn vanilla essence [extract]			
Fresh raspberries	225 g	8 oz	½ lb

Place the cream crackers in a polythene bag and crush with a rolling pin. Whisk the egg whites until frothy. Gradually whisk in the 6 oz/175 g sugar and the baking powder. Continue whisking until very stiff peaks form. Fold in the cracker crumbs and chopped walnuts. Pile into a lightly greased 10 inch/25 cm flan dish. Bake in a moderate oven (350°F, 180°C, Gas Mark 4) for 30-35 minutes. Let cool. Whisk the cream lightly, gradually add one teaspoon of the sugar and the vanilla essence. Spoon the remaining sugar over the fresh raspberries. Fold the raspberries into the whipped cream. Spoon over the meringue. Refrigerate until serving time. Serves 8.

Left-over turkey is delicious served with cream sauces, fruity sauces, or sautéed with nuts. Fold chopped cooked turkey into a savoury white or cheese sauce, and serve over rice. Add a pinch of curry powder to a white sauce, with plenty of lemon juice to sharpen the flavour, or cinnamon and orange juice for a sweeter, spicy flavour. For quite a different texture, sauté the chopped turkey in butter and oil, with a seasoning of salt and black pepper, sometimes using celery or garlic salt. Add roughly chopped nuts, such as hazelnuts, walnuts, almonds or peanuts for an extra minute at the end of cooking.

MENU 31

Honeyed spare ribs
Special fried rice
Orange sundaes flambées

Honeyed spare ribs

INGREDIENTS	METRIC	IMP.	U.S.
Pork spare ribs	1.5 kg	3 lbs	3 lbs
Salt			
Clear honey	4 tbspn	4 tbspn	5 tbspn
2 tbspn soy sauce			
1 tbspn lemon juice			
½ tspn ground ginger			
Canned pineapple chunks	225 g	8 oz	8 oz
Vinegar	4 tbspn	4 tbspn	5 tbspn
1 small sweet red pepper			
1 onion			

Cut the pork into separate ribs and place in a large roasting tin. Sprinkle with salt and cook in a moderately hot oven (375°F, 190°C, Gas Mark 5) for 45 minutes, pouring off the fat as it collects. At the same time, gently melt the honey in a small saucepan together with the soy sauce, lemon juice and ginger. Lower oven heat to moderate (325°F, 170°C, Gas Mark 3), pour half the honey mixture evenly over the ribs and continue cooking for another 30 minutes, or until the ribs are well browned.

Meanwhile drain the pineapple and add pineapple syrup and vinegar to the rest of the honey mixture. Deseed the red pepper and cut into chunks. Cut the onion into strips. Poach the pepper and onion in the honey mixture for 8 minutes, add the pineapple and cook for a further 2 minutes. Place spare ribs and sauce in a hot serving dish.

Special fried rice Cook 225 g/8 oz/1 cup long grain rice in plenty of boiling salted water until just tender, drain and rinse with fresh water in a colander. Drain again and cool. Melt a large knob of butter in a shallow saucepan, add the rice and fry until turning colour. Add 2 tablespoons chopped prawns, 2 tablespoons cooked chopped button mushrooms and 1 hardboiled egg, chopped. Stir through the rice over moderate heat until hot. Serve at once.

Orange sundaes flambées

INGREDIENTS	METRIC	IMP.	U.S.
3 large oranges			
Chopped dates	25 g	1 oz	¼ cup
Orange juice	125 ml	4 fl oz	½ cup
8 scoops vanilla ice cream			
Toasted flaked almonds	25 g	1 oz	¼ cup
2 tbspn Cointreau			
2 tbspn brandy			

Peel the oranges, removing all the white pith. Dice the orange flesh and combine with the chopped dates and orange juice. Allow to stand for 1 hour. At serving time, pile up the scoops of ice cream in a serving-dish. Pour the orange and date sauce into a chafing dish and heat until slightly thickened. Stir in the toasted almonds. Warm the Cointreau and brandy. Pour over the sauce and ignite. Ladle the flaming orange sauce over the ice cream.

Pâté de foie gras with aspic
Roast turkey with
chestnut and lemon stuffing
Roast potatoes   Russian salad
Bûche de Noël

Bûche de Noël

INGREDIENTS	METRIC	IMP.	U.S.
3 eggs			
Castor [granulated] sugar	100 g	4 oz	½ cup
Few drops vanilla essence [extract]			
Self-raising flour [all-purpose flour + ¾ tspn baking powder]	75 g	3 oz	¾ cup
Melted butter	25 g	1 oz	2 tbspn
1 tbspn hot water			
Icing [confectioner's] sugar to sprinkle			
BUTTER CREAM			
Plain [unsweetened] chocolate	25 g	1 oz	1 square
1 tspn instant coffee			
1 tspn boiling water			
Softened butter	75 g	3 oz	⅓ cup
Icing [confectioner's] sugar	175 g	6 oz	1½ cups
CHOCOLATE LEAVES			
Plain [unsweetened] chocolate	225 g	8 oz	8 squares

8–12 even-sized unblemished rose leaves or other
similar shape evergreen leaves

Russian salad Combine 6 tablespoons thick
mayonnaise with 3 tablespoons whipped cream. Mix
together 6 tablespoons each cooked peas, diced
carrot, diced potato and chopped green beans. Fold in
the mayonnaise mixture. Spoon the salad into lettuce
leaf cups on 6 small side dishes.

Pâté de foie gras with aspic Make up 600 ml/
1 pint/2½ cups clear aspic jelly, using chicken stock
(broth) and gelatine if needed. Pour into a baking tray,
so that it covers the bottom about 1 cm/½ inch deep.
Allow to set. Cut in parallel lines with a sharp knife
both ways to make small squares. Arrange 6 slices of
pâté on 6 small plates and garnish with the diced aspic
jelly. Serve with freshly made hot toast and butter.

Whisk the eggs, sugar and vanilla essence together until thick and pale in colour. Sift the
flour and gradually fold in, then fold in the
melted butter and hot water. Pour the mixture into a Swiss roll (jelly roll) tin lined with non-stick
cooking parchment. Bake in a hot oven (425°F,
220°C, Gas Mark 7) for 8-10 minutes, until
well risen and pale golden in colour. Turn out on
another sheet of cooking parchment and strip off
the sheet used in cooking. Make a cut 2.5 cm/
1 inch from the end of the cake across one short
side to make it easier to roll the cake. Roll up the
cake and parchment together and leave to cool.
To make the filling, melt the chocolate and dissolve the coffee in the boiling water. Cream the
butter and sugar together until smooth, add the
chocolate and coffee and beat until creamy,
adding a very little milk if necessary. Unroll the
cake, spread with a layer of the butter cream and
re-roll it. Place on a serving dish and cover all
over with the remaining butter cream. Using a
fork make lines along the surface to resemble the
bark of a tree, and make circular lines at each
end. Chill. To make the chocolate leaves, melt
the chocolate and use to coat the under-sides of
the leaves with a smooth layer. Leave to cool and
set on a sheet of parchment. When cold and set,
gently peel off the leaves and place the chocolate
shapes with the veined sides upwards in a decorative pattern on the bûche. Sift the top with
icing sugar and serve, arranging any extra chocolate leaves round the base. Serves 6.

Roast turkey with chestnut and lemon stuffing

INGREDIENTS	METRIC	IMP.	U.S.
1 turkey	3-4 kg	6-8 lb	6-8 lb
STUFFING			
3 rashers [slices] bacon			
Chestnuts	450 g	1 lb	1 lb
Fresh white breadcrumbs	100 g	4 oz	1½ cups
1 tbspn chopped parsley			
Grated rind 1 lemon			
Salt and pepper			
1 egg, beaten			

Remove the rind from the bacon and chop. Fry gently for about 4 minutes, until crisp, and most of the fat is rendered out. Boil the chestnuts for 5 minutes to loosen the skins, cool and peel. Cook in boiling salted water until tender. Reserve a few for garnishing the turkey, and sieve the remainder. Mix together with all the other ingredients and use to stuff the neck end of the turkey. (If chestnuts are not required whole to garnish, 100 g/4 oz/½ cup canned chestnut purée can be used instead.) Roast the turkey in a moderate oven (350°F, 180°C, Gas Mark 4) for about 2½-3 hours, depending on weight. Serves 6.

MENU
33

Canterbury cocktail
Pork chops with Brussels sprouts
and onion rice
Crème brûlée

Canterbury cocktail

INGREDIENTS	METRIC	IMP.	U.S.
1 large orange			
Juice of 1 lemon			
Corn [salad] oil	175 ml	6 fl oz	¾ cup
2 tspn sugar			
1 tbspn chopped mint or tarragon			
Salt and pepper			
3 ripe tomatoes			
2 ripe Conference pears			
4 red dessert apples			
1 tbspn lemon juice			
Sprigs of mint			

Grate the rind from the orange and extract the juice. Mix the orange juice with the lemon juice, oil, sugar, chopped herbs and seasoning. Pour into a deep bowl. Skin the tomatoes and sieve the pulp into the orange dressing, discarding the seeds. Chop the flesh and add to the dressing. Peel, core and chop the pears and three of the apples. Add to the orange dressing. Chill. To serve, spoon into 4 dishes. Slice the remaining apple and dip in the lemon juice. Arrange over each cocktail and sprinkle with the grated orange rind and sprigs of fresh mint.

Pork chops with Brussels sprouts and onion rice

INGREDIENTS	METRIC	IMP.	U.S.
Brussels sprouts	450 g	1 lb	1 lb
Butter	50 g	2 oz	¼ cup
Salt and pepper			
4 large pork chops			
2 tbspn cold water			
Chopped parsley			
ONION RICE			
1 large onion			
Butter	50 g	2 oz	¼ cup
Long grain rice	225 g	8 oz	1 cup
Water	600 ml	1 pint	2½ cups
1 tspn salt			

First prepare the onion rice. Chop the onion and fry lightly in the butter until golden. Add the rice and stir over heat for 1 minute. Add the water and salt, mix again and bring to the boil. Stir once, cover and simmer for 15 minutes, or until the rice is tender and the liquid absorbed. Cook the Brussels sprouts in boiling salted water. When they are cooked but still firm, drain well and place in a pan with half the butter. Season with pepper, cover and cook for 10 minutes. Meanwhile season the chops and place in a pan with the remaining butter. Cook over moderate heat for 5–6 minutes on each side depending on thickness. Place on a hot serving dish, surround with the sprouts and onion rice. Add 2 tablespoons cold water to the pan juices from cooking the chops. Stir well and bring to the boil. Spoon over the chops and sprinkle with parsley.

Crème brûlée

INGREDIENTS	METRIC	IMP.	U.S.
Single cream [half & half]	600 ml	1 pint	2½ cups
4 egg yolks			
Castor [granulated] sugar	25 g	1 oz	2 tbspn
1-2 drops vanilla essence [extract]			
TOPPING			
Soft [light] brown sugar			

Place the cream in a saucepan and bring almost to the boil, then remove from the heat. Put the egg yolks and sugar in a bowl and blend together. Stirring, pour on the cream and add the vanilla essence. Strain the mixture into a 6 inch/15 cm soufflé dish, place in a bain marie and bake in a moderate oven (350°F, 180°C, Gas Mark 4) 45 minutes or until firm. Remove from the oven and leave to cool. Sprinkle the surface with a layer of soft brown sugar and place under a fully heated grill to allow the sugar to caramelise. Serve at once.

MENU 34

Sunburst artichokes
Roast lamb with flageolets
Pommes Parisienne
Figs with almond stuffing

Sunburst artichokes

INGREDIENTS	METRIC	IMP.	U.S.
4 globe artichokes			
Mayonnaise	300 ml	½ pint	1¼ cups
1 tbspn prepared mustard			
1 tbspn lemon juice			
Salt and pepper			
4 hard-boiled eggs			
Chopped parsley			

Plunge the artichokes into boiling salted water and boil gently for 30 minutes. Drain, trim off the points of the leaves and the stalk from the bottom. Chill. Mix the mayonnaise, mustard, lemon juice and salt and pepper to taste. Slice each hard-boiled egg into 8 wedges. Pull out the centre leaves and 'choke' from each artichoke and spoon some of the mayonnaise mixture into the centres. Arrange 8 egg wedges around each artichoke. Top with remaining mayonnaise and chopped parsley.

Roast lamb with flageolets

INGREDIENTS	METRIC	IMP.	U.S.
1 small leg of lamb			
2 cloves garlic			
2 tbspn oil			
Salt and pepper			
3 sprigs rosemary			
Canned flageolets [lima beans]	425 g	15 oz	15 oz
Beef stock [broth]	150 ml	¼ pint	½ cup

Slash the surface of the joint diagonally into diamonds. Cut the cloves of garlic into slivers and insert at the points of the diamonds. Brush with oil, sprinkle with salt and pepper and lay 1 sprig of rosemary on top. Roast in a moderately hot oven (375°F, 190°C, Gas Mark 5) for 1½ hours, or until cooked through. Place on a warm serving dish, remove the sprig of rosemary and arrange tiny fresh sprigs of rosemary over the top of the joint. Keep hot. Drain the flageolets in a colander and rinse with fresh cold water. Heat in the stock. Remove with a slotted draining spoon, arrange round the joint and use the stock to make gravy.

Pommes Parisienne

INGREDIENTS	METRIC	IMP.	U.S.
Large potatoes	1 kg	2 lb	2 lb
Butter	50 g	2 oz	¼ cup
1 tbspn oil			
Salt			

Peel the potatoes. Using a round vegetable baller, scoop small balls from the potatoes. Boil them until just tender, then drain well. Heat the butter and oil in a frying pan, add the potato balls and fry briskly, turning frequently, until golden brown all over. Sprinkle with salt and arrange round the leg of lamb with the flageolets.

Figs with almond stuffing

INGREDIENTS	METRIC	IMP.	U.S.
8 large figs			
Ground almonds	50 g	2 oz	½ cup
Icing [confectioner's] sugar	50 g	2 oz	¼ cup
1 small Petit Suisse [2 tbspn cream] cheese			
8 whole almonds			

Cut the figs in half almost through to the base and again at right angles, so that they open out into four 'petals'. Beat together the ground almonds, sieved icing sugar and the cheese. Fill the centres of the figs with this mixture and decorate with whole almonds.

Herb tartlets
Pheasant in brandy sauce
Scalloped potatoes
Violet ice cream

Herb tartlets

INGREDIENTS	METRIC	IMP.	U.S.
Shortcrust pastry [basic pie dough]	350 g	12 oz	$\frac{3}{4}$ lb
Curd [farmer] cheese	150 g	5 oz	$\frac{3}{4}$ cup
2 eggs, beaten			
1 tbspn chopped chives			
Salt and pepper			

Roll out the pastry thinly, cut out circles with a fluted biscuit cutter and use to line 8 patty tins. Bake blind in a moderately hot oven (375°F, 190°C, Gas Mark 5) for 10 minutes. Meanwhile, beat the cheese until smooth, then gradually add the eggs, chives and seasoning to taste. Divide the filling between the 8 tartlet cases and return to the oven for 20 minutes, until well risen and brown.

Pheasant in brandy sauce

INGREDIENTS	METRIC	IMP.	U.S.
1 young pheasant			
1 small onion			
Pheasant liver			
Streaky [side] bacon slices	50 g	2 oz	2 oz
2 tbspn oil			
Butter	25 g	1 oz	2 tbspn
4 tbspn brandy			
Sliced mushrooms	100 g	4 oz	1 cup
Red wine	300 ml	½ pint	1¼ cups
Salt and freshly ground black pepper			
Double [whipping] cream	150 ml	¼ pint	⅔ cup
Watercress sprigs and fried bread triangles to garnish			

Prepare the pheasant. Chop the onion finely and mix with the chopped pheasant liver. Put the mixture inside the pheasant. Remove the bacon rinds and chop the rashers finely. Place in a heavy, flameproof pan and heat until the fat runs. Increase the heat to brown the chopped bacon. Remove the bacon and keep aside. Add the oil and butter to the fat remaining in the pan, heat and brown the pheasant on all sides. Warm the brandy and pour it over the pheasant. Ignite and shake the pan backwards and forwards until the flames subside. Return the bacon to the pan, add the mushrooms, wine and seasoning. Cover tightly and simmer for 1 hour. Arrange the pheasant on a serving dish and keep hot. Place the flameproof casserole on the heat and whisk in the cream. Whisk over a moderate heat until the sauce is smooth. Check the seasoning, then pour over the pheasant and serve garnished with sprigs of watercress and triangles of fried bread.

Note: Triangles of bread may be prepared and fried in advance and stored in a polythene container in the freezer to serve with this and other game or poultry casseroles.

Scalloped potatoes Cut 750 g/1½ lb potatoes into very thin slices. Dissolve a chicken stock (bouillon) cube in 300 ml/½ pint/1¼ cups water and place in a saucepan. Add the potatoes, bring to the boil, cover and cook for about 5 minutes. Drain and place in a greased ovenproof dish. Season well, pour over 150 ml/¼ pint/½ cup single cream (half and half), sprinkle with 4 tablespoons grated cheese and a little paprika pepper. Bake in a moderately hot oven (375°F, 190°C, Gas Mark 5) for 45 minutes.

Violet ice cream

INGREDIENTS	METRIC	IMP.	U.S.
Fresh brown breadcrumbs	75 g	3 oz	1¼ cups
1 tbspn orange juice			
3 tbspn clear honey			
Crystallised [candied] violets	25 g	1 oz	2 tbspn
Double [whipping] cream	300 ml	½ pint	1¼ cups
2 tspn castor [granulated] sugar			

Crumble the bread very finely. Warm the orange juice, dissolve the honey in it, and pour over the breadcrumbs. Allow to cool. Divide the violets in half, reserving the best ones for decoration, and crush the remainder with a rolling pin between layers of kitchen paper. Whip the cream with the sugar until thick, stir in the honey mixture and the crushed violets. Pour the mixture into a freezing tray, cover with foil or cling wrap, and freeze until crystals begin to form. Remove from the freezing tray and beat well, return to the tray and freeze until solid. Serve small portions, topping each with one or two of the reserved violets.

MENU
36

Cauliflower gratin
Chicken pimiento casserole
French bread and butter
Rhubarb and orange meringue

Cauliflower gratin

INGREDIENTS	METRIC	IMP.	U.S.
1 small cauliflower			
Butter	50 g	2 oz	4 tbspn
Flour	25 g	1 oz	2 tbspn
Milk	150 ml	¼ pint	⅔ cup
1 tbspn dry sherry			
Grated cheese	100 g	4 oz	1 cup
Peeled shrimps	50 g	2 oz	4 tbspns
2 egg yolks			
Mashed potato	225 g	8 oz	1 cup
Salt and pepper			
Good pinch nutmeg			

Remove outer leaves and core of cauliflower, break into sprigs, cook in enough boiling salted water to cover until tender, about 15 minutes. Drain and reserve a measured ¼ pint/150 ml/ ⅝ cup liquid for the sauce. Melt half the butter and use some of this to brush 4 deep shells or ramekin dishes. Use the remaining unmelted butter, flour, milk and reserved liquid to make a smooth sauce. Add the sherry, half the grated cheese and shrimps. Stir over low heat until cheese is melted, remove from heat and beat in one egg yolk. Taste and adjust the seasoning if necessary. Pour over the cauliflower. Beat the remaining egg yolk into the mashed potato, add nutmeg to taste, and pipe round the shells. Brush potato lightly with rest of melted butter. Sprinkle more grated cheese over the sauce. Place in a hot oven (425°F, 220°C, Gas Mark 7) for 20 minutes or until golden.

Chicken pimiento casserole

INGREDIENTS	METRIC	IMP.	U.S.
2 canned pimientoes			
Butter	75 g	3 oz	6 tbspn
Carrots, sliced	275 g	10 oz	2 cups
2 onions, chopped			
Quartered mushrooms	175 g	6 oz	1 cup +
4 chicken portions			
3 tbspn flour			
Salt and pepper			
1 tspn dried mixed herbs			
Chicken stock [broth]	750 ml	1¼ pints	3 cups +
Dry red wine	150 ml	¼ pint	½ cup +
1 tbspn chopped parsley			

Drain the pimientoes and cut into strips. Melt the butter in a flameproof casserole and use to fry the pimiento, carrot, onion and mushrooms together for a few minutes. Add the chicken portions and fry gently on both sides for about 5 minutes. Remove the chicken. Sprinkle in the flour, seasoning and herbs and stir thoroughly. Gradually add the stock, stirring constantly until thick. Add the wine and chicken, stir, bring to the boil, cover and simmer for 30-45 minutes. Turn the chicken once or twice during this time. Garnish with chopped parsley.

Rhubarb and orange meringue

INGREDIENTS	METRIC	IMP.	U.S.
Sliced rhubarb	100 g	4 oz	1 cup
Sugar	50 g	2 oz	4 tbspn
Packet orange blanc-mange powder	600 ml	1 pint	2½ cups
Milk	450 ml	¾ pint	2 cups
Canned mandarin oranges	300 g	11 oz	11 oz
Cake crumbs	225 g	8 oz	½ lb
2 eggs, separated			
Castor [granulated] sugar	100 g	4 oz	½ cup
Angelica			

Stew the rhubarb gently with 1 oz/25 g of the sugar and very little water, until tender, then purée. Place the blancmange powder and the remaining 1 oz/25 g sugar in a basin with 2 tablespoons of the milk. Heat the remaining milk then pour into the mixture, stir well and return to the saucepan. Bring to the boil, stirring constantly, and simmer for 3 minutes. Reserve a few mandarin segments for decoration and stir the remainder into the blancmange with the syrup from the can, the rhubarb purée, cake crumbs and egg yolks. Mix well and pour into an ovenproof dish. Whisk the egg whites until stiff, fold in the castor sugar and spoon or pipe the meringue over the fruit mixture. Brown in a moderately hot oven (375°F, 190°C, Gas Mark 5) for 10–15 minutes. Decorate with reserved mandarin segments and pieces of angelica.

MENU
37

Smoked cod's roe cream
Melba toast
Chicken in sour cream
Tossed green salad
Fruited savarin

Smoked cod's roe cream

INGREDIENTS	METRIC	IMP.	U.S.
3 slices white bread			
Water	50 ml	2 fl oz	$\frac{1}{4}$ cup
Smoked cod's roe	225 g	8 oz	$\frac{1}{2}$ lb
1 small onion, grated			
Freshly ground black pepper			
Juice of 1 lemon			
Oil	4 tbspn	4 tbspn	$\frac{1}{3}$ cup
Double [whipping] cream	4 tbspn	4 tbspn	$\frac{1}{3}$ cup
Few black olives			

Remove crusts from the bread and soak in the water. Skin the cod's roe and pound with the onion and soaked bread, pepper to taste, the lemon juice and oil to make a smooth paste. Gradually beat in the cream. Spoon into 4 small ramekin dishes and chill. Garnish with halved and stoned olives and serve with Melba toast.

Chicken in sour cream

INGREDIENTS	METRIC	IMP.	U.S.
Butter	25 g	1 oz	2 tbspn
Chopped lean bacon	100 g	4 oz	¼ lb
1 large onion, chopped			
4 chicken portions			
Salt and pepper			
1 chicken stock [bouillon] cube			
Boiling water	450 ml	¾ pint	2 cups
2 bay leaves			
Red wine	150 ml	¼ pint	⅔ cup
½ lemon			
SAUCE			
Butter	25 g	1 oz	2 tbspn
Flour	25 g	1 oz	¼ cup
Mushrooms	100 g	4 oz	¼ lb
Soured cream	150 ml	¼ pint	⅔ cup

Melt the butter and use to sauté the bacon and onion until golden. Transfer to a deep ovenproof casserole and place the chicken portions on top. Season with salt and pepper. Make up the stock cube with the boiling water and pour into the casserole. Add the bay leaves, wine, juice of the half lemon and the squeezed lemon half. Cover and cook in a moderate oven (350°F, 180°C, Gas Mark 4) for about 1 hour. Strain off the stock from the casserole. To make the sauce, melt the butter in a saucepan and stir in the flour. Gradually add the strained stock and bring to the boil, stirring constantly. Add the mushrooms and cook for 5 minutes. Remove from the heat and stir in the soured cream. Pour the sauce over the chicken portions, remove the lemon half, and serve.

Fruited savarin

INGREDIENTS	METRIC	IMP.	U.S.
Fresh yeast, or 2 tspn dried yeast	15 g	½ oz	1 tbspn
Warm milk	150 ml	¼ pint	½ cup+
Plain [all-purpose] flour	150 g	5 oz	1¼ cups
¼ tspn salt			
Castor [granulated] sugar	15 g	½ oz	1 tbspn
1 egg, beaten			
Butter	25 g	1 oz	2 tbspn
Quartered glacé [candied] cherries	50 g	2 oz	½ cup
Sultanas [golden raisins]	50 g	2 oz	½ cup −
Seedless raisins	50 g	2 oz	½ cup −
Little butter for greasing tin			
Flaked [slivered] almonds	15 g	½ oz	2 tbspn
SYRUP			
Granulated sugar	225 g	8 oz	1 cup
Water	300 ml	½ pint	1¼ cups
2 tbspn sweet sherry			
Double [whipping] cream	150 ml	¼ pint	½ cup

Combine the yeast, milk and 1 oz/25 g flour in a large bowl, beat until smooth then leave until frothy, about 20 minutes for fresh yeast, 30 minutes for dried yeast. Add remaining flour, salt, castor sugar, egg and softened butter to the yeast mixture and, using a wooden spoon, beat thoroughly for 3-4 minutes. Stir in the cherries, sultanas and raisins. Grease a 7 inch/18 cm ring mould with a little butter and sprinkle with the almonds. Spoon mixture into the mould and cover with foil or polythene. Allow to rise in a warm place for about 45 minutes to 1 hour, until mixture almost reaches the top of the mould. Bake in a moderately hot oven (400°F, 200°C, Gas Mark 6) for about 25 minutes, until firm to the touch and golden brown. Remove from the oven and leave in the mould for 5 minutes, turn out on a wire rack to cool. To make the syrup, dissolve the granulated sugar in the water, boil for 2 minutes. Remove from the heat and stir in the sherry. Return savarin to the mould, spoon over half the syrup. Spoon over more syrup every 30 minutes until it has all been absorbed. Invert the mould on a serving dish and leave to stand for several hours, or overnight, until required. To serve, whip the cream until thick, remove mould from savarin and spoon the cream into the centre.

Adding inspiration to vegetables

Very simple meat dishes can be transformed into quite a banquet by serving an elaborate vegetable dish. Or, with a little loving care and attention, vegetables themselves can be turned into a main course. Here are some ideas to make the everyday favourites from the supermarket shelves rather more special.

Serve broccoli with a white sauce flavoured with curry powder

Serve cauliflower with a blue cheese sauce

Sauté almonds in butter and add to cooked green beans

Garnish celery cooked in stock with grated cheese

Glaze parsnips with melted honey and butter

Toss Brussels sprouts in a seasoned butter made by adding lemon juice, dried oregano, crushed garlic, salt and pepper to the butter

Pour condensed cream of mushroom soup over cooked carrots, top with fried onion rings and bake in a moderate oven until hot and bubbly

Diced cucumber with herb butter

INGREDIENTS	METRIC	IMP.	U.S.
1 large cucumber			
1 tsp salt			
Butter	25 g	1 oz	2 tbspn
1 tbspn chopped fresh herbs such as parsley, mint and thyme			

Cut the unpeeled cucumber into cubes and sprinkle with salt. Leave aside for 1 hour, then strain off the excess juices. Heat the butter in a frying pan and sauté the drained cucumber for 2 minutes over low heat. Add the chopped herbs.

Ratatouille Lavandaise

INGREDIENTS	METRIC	IMP.	U.S.
Aubergines [eggplants]	450 g	1 lb	1 lb
Salt			
Olive oil	4 tbspn	4 tbspn	⅓ cup
1 large onion, sliced			
1 medium green [sweet] pepper			
1 medium red [sweet] pepper			
Courgettes [zucchini]	450 g	1 lb	1 lb
4 tomatoes			
1 tspn dried thyme			
¼ tspn dried basil			
Salt and pepper			

Slice the aubergines and sprinkle with salt. Leave aside for 1 hour, then drain off the liquid. Dry on absorbent paper. Heat half the oil in a large frying pan and lightly fry the sliced onion. Add the remaining oil to the pan together with the seeded and sliced peppers and sliced courgettes. Continue frying gently, turning the mixture from time to time. Add the aubergines, skinned and sliced tomatoes, herbs and seasonings. Cook for a further 20-25 minutes.

Fennel with black olive dressing

INGREDIENTS	METRIC	IMP.	U.S.
Button mushrooms	100 g	4 oz	1 cup
8 black olives			
4 spring onions [scallions], trimmed			
2 tbspn wine vinegar			
Salt and pepper			
1 tspn mild continental mustard			
4 tbspn oil			
1 small head fennel, trimmed			
2 tbspn double [whipping] cream			
1 tbspn chopped mint			

Slice the mushrooms thinly, halve and stone the olives, and chop the onions. Whisk together the vinegar, salt, pepper, mustard and oil. Put all together in an airtight container in the refrigerator for at least 2 hours, turning once. Cut the fennel in quarters, and cook in lightly salted boiling water until just tender, about 15 minutes. Drain well and cool. Divide the fennel quarters between 4 individual serving dishes. Whisk the cream into the mushroom mixture and spoon it over the fennel. Sprinkle with chopped mint and serve chilled.

Couronne de legumes

INGREDIENTS	METRIC	IMP.	U.S.
Green beans	450 g	1 lb	1 lb
Baby carrots	450 g	1 lb	1 lb
2 large leeks			
Button onions	225 g	8 oz	½ lb
2 small turnips			
1 celery heart			
2 medium potatoes			
Butter	40 g	1½ oz	3 tbspns
Salt and pepper			
Savoury white sauce	600 ml	1 pint	2½ cups
Grated Gruyère [Swiss] cheese	100 g	4 oz	1 cup
2 eggs separated			

Peel all the vegetables and cut into strips, reserving a few nice ones whole for the centre of the ring. Toss all the vegetables in the butter over low heat, and season lightly. Reserve the whole vegetables and keep hot. Mix the chopped ones with the sauce, cheese and the egg yolks. Cool. Whisk the egg whites stiffly and fold into the mixture. Turn into a well-greased ring mould and cook in a moderately hot oven (375°F, 190°C, Gas Mark 5) for about 30 minutes until golden brown. Turn out on a warm serving dish and fill the centre with the reserved vegetables.

Marrow snack

INGREDIENTS	METRIC	IMP.	U.S.
1 small vegetable marrow [summer squash]			
Streaky [side] bacon slices	100 g	4 oz	4 oz
Butter	25 g	1 oz	2 tbspns
1 tspn ground turmeric			
Salt and pepper			
Finely grated rind of 1 orange			
1 tbspn browned breadcrumbs			

Peel the marrow, cut into 1 inch/2.5 cm rings, remove pith and cut each ring into quarters. Par-boil in salted water for about 5 minutes, drain well. Meanwhile derind the bacon and cut each rasher into three. Roll up and thread on two skewers. Place in a shallow ovenproof dish in a moderately hot oven (375°F, 190°C, Gas Mark 5). When the bacon rolls are crisp, slide off the skewers and keep hot. Melt the butter in the rendered bacon fat, stir in the turmeric, salt, pepper and orange rind. Turn the marrow quarters lightly in the mixture, sprinkle the bacon rolls and breadcrumbs on top and return to the oven for 15 minutes. Serve very hot.

Acknowledgments
The author and publishers thank the following for their help
in supplying photographs for this book, some of which
were adapted from Four Seasons Cookery:
Thorn Domestic Appliances (Electrical) Ltd., p. 16-17
California Wine Institute, p. 18-19, p. 24-25
The Mushroom Information Bureau, p. 28-29
Kraft Foods Ltd., p. 28-29
Bakewell Non-stick Cooking Parchment, p. 30-31, p. 78-79
Knorr, p. 32-33
The Home Baking Bureau, p. 34-35
Buxted Brand Products by Ross Poultry Ltd., p. 36-37,
    p. 42-43, p. 50-51, p. 54-55, p. 86-87
Colman's Mustard, p. 38-39
New Zealand Lamb Information Bureau, p. 40-41, p. 58-59
James Robertson & Sons (Preserve Manufacturers) Ltd.,
    p. 44-45
U.S. Rice Council, p. 46-47, p. 80-81
Trex by Princes Foods Ltd., p. 56-57
The Tupperware Company, p. 58-59
The Apple and Pear Development Council, p. 60-61,
    p. 80-81
British Sugar Bureau, p. 62-63
The Carnation Milk Bureau, p. 62-63, 68-69
John West Foods, p. 64-65, p. 82-83
Tabasco Pepper Sauce, p. 72-73
Wall's Ice Cream, p. 72-73
Olives from Spain, p. 74-75
Gale's Honey, p. 76-77
British Turkey Federation, p. 78-79
Brown & Polson Patent Cornflour, p. 86-87

92

Index